Scope of Work

Readers of this text may be interested in the following publications from the Appraisal Institute:

- *The Appraisal of Real Estate*, twelfth edition
- *The Dictionary of Real Estate Appraisal*, fourth edition

Appraisal
Institute®
*Professionals Providing
Real Estate Solutions*

Scope of Work

by Stephanie Coleman, MAI, SRA

Appraisal Institute · 550 West Van Buren · Chicago, IL 60607 · appraisalinstitute.org

Reviewers: Peter D. Bowes, MAI
Richard Marchitelli, MAI
John Schwartz, MAI

*Vice President, Educational Programs
and Publications:* Larisa Phillips
Director, Publications: Stephanie Shea-Joyce
Editor: Mark Boone
Manager, Book Design/Production: Michael Landis
Production Specialist: James Sobiesczyk

For Educational Purposes Only

Nondiscrimination Policy

Library of Congress Cataloging-in-Publication Data

Coleman, Stephanie C.
Scope of work / Stephanie Coleman, MAI, SRA.
    p. cm.
ISBN 0-922154-88-0
1. Real property–Valuation. I. Title
HD1387.C613 2006
333.33'2–dc22

2006042720

Table of Contents

The appraisal business is a service business. As such, an appraiser's concern is how to fulfill a client's need for meaningful, well-reasoned answers to questions about property value. The appraiser's role in this process is to be unbiased, objective, and impartial when rendering an opinion.

In the last decade, the *Uniform Standards of Professional Appraisal Practice* (USPAP) has evolved from a document that lists a series of "musts" for the appraiser to apply in the appraisal process, to one that emphasizes the appraiser's application of sound judgment in solving the problem at hand. The new USPAP stresses that, to arrive at a credible solution, the practitioner must properly identify the problem to be solved, identify the appropriate way to solve it, and competently apply the solution. The ability to make these judgments is the hallmark of a true professional.

Scope of Work is intended to raise awareness among appraisers. It explains that USPAP provides the flexibility to perform a variety of appraisal services and describes how those services can be performed without compromising objectivity and impartiality. Illustrations and examples are presented to demonstrate ways in which appraisers can apply the scope of work concept and communicate it effectively in a report. This book examines the structure of USPAP and the way in which scope of work applies within the Standards Rules. It also addresses the range of services that a real property appraiser can offer and the practical application of scope of work in a variety of appraisal assignments. The overall objective of *Scope of Work* is to help appraisers customize their work products and provide their clients with services that meet their needs.

Richard D. Powers, MAI, SRA
2006 Appraisal Institute President

Stephanie Coleman, MAI, SRA, is the Director of Screening for the Appraisal Institute. She has nearly 30 years of experience in the property valuation field and has been actively involved with the Appraisal Institute in the areas of appraisal standards, ethics and counseling, education, and publications. She is the author of *Understanding Limited Appraisals and Appraisal Reporting Options,* published by the Appraisal Institute in 1994, and co-developed a seminar by the same name. More recently, she has been involved in the development of the Appraisal Institute's Scope of Work seminar. Ms. Coleman is a past member of the Appraisal Standards Board of The Appraisal Foundation, the body responsible for developing and interpreting the Uniform Standards of Professional Appraisal Practice (USPAP). She is an AQB-certified USPAP instructor and is actively engaged in teaching classes on USPAP throughout the United States.

Introduction

Throughout the history of civilization, rules have existed in many forms. Spoken or unspoken, rules have always been a necessary part of human life, aiding in efforts to organize, maintain, and advance. There are rules that govern the behavior of individuals within society. There are rules for implementing processes of all types, from the way warfare is conducted to the way traffic flows. There are rules to achieve stated outcomes, including everything from the rules of astronautical engineering that govern the construction of rockets to be propelled into outer space to rules that govern how ball games and board games are played.

Two statements are commonly made about rules. First, rules are made to be broken. Second, there are exceptions to every rule. We will not comment of the first–except to say that if the second is true, the first is probably not true. That is, if exceptions are allowed when appropriate, there should never be any need to break the rules.

Imagine writing a set of rules for some activity–any activity, whether it be, say, mixing a cocktail, sky diving, or writing a doctoral dissertation. In writing such rules, you might find it necessary to include some type of exception clause, some way of making reasonable exceptions from the rules when such exceptions are appropriate. If you didn't, you'd likely find that the rules would not be workable in all circumstances, and they'd end up being broken.

This is the reason the Departure Rule (originally called the Departure Provision) was included in the Uniform Standards of Professional Appraisal Practice (USPAP). The creators of USPAP–the generally recognized standards of appraisal practice in the United States–saw the need to allow exceptions to the rules they set forth when such exceptions were reasonable and appropriate.

The Departure Rule was intended to be the primary mechanism for flexibility in USPAP. It allowed appraisers to do something less than the work required by certain Standards Rules, as long as doing less did not yield assignment results that weren't credible, and as long as appropriate disclosures were made regarding the exceptions.

In theory, departure was a simple—yet sufficient—mechanism. In practice, it proved to be problematic. Hence, beginning in 1999, the Appraisal Standards Board (ASB) of the Appraisal Foundation began to introduce a replacement concept—scope of work. In 2005, the ASB finalized changes to USPAP regarding scope of work. These changes are effective July 1, 2006.

Scope of work is now the primary mechanism for flexibility in USPAP. It gives appraisers the ability to tailor each assignment appropriately for the circumstances. Understanding scope of work can lead to new business opportunities for the appraiser and it can also increase client satisfaction.

However, flexibility comes at the price of increased responsibility. Scope of work is a useful and powerful tool when handled by the competent professional. If the tool is misused, the results can be disastrous. The appraiser must give careful thought to the scope of work decision, must be prepared to defend that decision, and must clearly explain the scope of work of an assignment in any report.

About This Book

Scope of Work is intended to raise awareness about how USPAP allows appraisers the flexibility to provide a variety of services. Illustrations and examples are included to show how to apply the scope of work concept in practice and how to communicate it effectively in a report. This book examines the structure of USPAP to understand how the concept works with the standards rules. It then addresses the range of services a real property appraiser can offer and the practical application of scope of work in a variety of appraisal assignments. The intent is to assist appraisers in customizing their work and providing their clients with services that satisfy their needs.

Given the vast amount of change the appraisal industry has faced in recent years, most appraisers would probably prefer to see appraisal standards and requirements remain

Note that while scope of work applies also to personal property appraising, mass appraising, business valuation, and appraisal consulting assignments, this text focuses on the appraisal of real property.

static for a while to allow time for us to catch our breath and fully grasp how far the profession has come to date. Unfortunately, this is not and cannot be the case. Rather, the appraisal profession will continue to evolve in the foreseeable future, and those who wish to remain part of the industry must be prepared to accept that fact.

The standards themselves are continuously being revised by the ASB. The ASB is likely to issue further communications providing new definitions of terms or detailed explanations about recent revisions to USPAP. Appraisers must remain alert for further communications from the ASB concerning their interpretations. Readers are also cautioned to remain aware of the laws governing the activities of appraisers in the state or states in which they practice. Each state has its own appraisal regulatory agency, and although federal law mandates that all state appraisal laws be subject to federal oversight, there are variations among the states' requirements and interpretations.

Finally, the Appraisal Institute has not yet fully adopted policies for admissions and review and counseling on this subject. Members and affiliates are urged to watch for changes in these areas as they develop. Such changes will be reported in *Appraiser News Online.*

Chapter 1

"The chief cause of problems is solutions."–Eric Sevareid

Appraisers are problem solvers, and appraisal practice involves solving problems. These problems arise because clients have questions or concerns about the value of property. They turn to appraisers for their expertise in property valuation because appraisers certify that their work is unbiased, impartial, and objective. Independence is the hallmark of a professional appraiser and is critically important to clients who need solutions they can rely on.

The appraiser's approach to solving a valuation problem is in many ways no different from the approach that anyone might use to solve any problem. All day, every day, people from all walks of life encounter problems of all sorts, challenges that need to be overcome, questions that need to be answered, and puzzles that require solving. Effective problem solving always involves the following three steps:

1. Identify the problem.
2. Plan the solution.
3. Apply the solution.

These steps are the same regardless of the nature of the problem. Consider the following examples:

Table 1.1: Problem-solving Steps

The Situation	Step 1 Identify the problem.	Step 2 Plan the solution.	Step 3 Apply the solution.
Your old car has reached the end of its useful life.	You need a new car.	Go on-line and research car makes and models. Arrange financing. Find local dealers. Negotiate.	Do it! Buy a new car.
Your patient has a broken arm.	The x-ray shows a complete fracture of the ulna.	Perform surgery to set the bones. Immobilize the arm. Prescribe physical therapy to begin in six weeks.	Do it! Fix the broken arm.
Your family has gotten bigger, but your house has not.	You need another bedroom.	Hire an architect. See what zoning will allow. Review alternative plans. Arrange financing.	Do it! Get that room addition.
You have 20 guests showing up for a backyard barbecue in 20 minutes.	Wasps and bees have arrived en masse.	Spray aggressively with XYZ bug repellent. Set out large fans. Hope for the best.	Do it! Host the party.

The first step, identifying the problem, is often much more difficult than it appears on the surface. We may have a preconceived notion about the nature of the problem. We might think we know what the problem is, when we really don't. Perhaps we believe what we wish to be true, just because we happen to have–or happen to like–a certain solution. For example, in the new car scenario, maybe the problem isn't really that it's time to say good-bye to your old car. Maybe with a tune-up, a few new parts, and some bodywork, your old car can be on the road again. Maybe replacing it with a new car is an extravagant solution. Or, maybe you want a new car far more than you need one.

The second step, planning the solution, can be tricky if there are few possible solutions. As the saying goes, "if the only tool you have is a hammer, everything starts to look like a nail." The hammer is not going to help you much if what you're looking at is not a nail, but a piece of glass.

Likewise, being confronted with too many possible solutions can be treacherous. The greater the number of possible solutions, the greater the risk that the course of action selected will be the wrong one.

Being able to pick the right solution implies a certain level of knowledge and expertise. You need to know enough about the situation to know that there *is* a problem, let alone how to solve it. And how do you know when you don't know enough? Therein lies the dilemma. Not knowing enough about the problem virtually guarantees that the approach you choose to solve it will be the wrong one–unless you are simply lucky. It is an age-old conundrum.

The problem-solving paradigm applies equally well to appraisal practice. Here are some common scenarios:

Table 1.2: Problem-solving with Appraisals			
The Situation	**Step 1** **Identify the problem.**	**Step 2** **Plan the solution.**	**Step 3** **Apply the solution.**
The client wants to sell his property, but he first needs to know how much it's worth.	How much would the property likely bring upon sale?	Inspect the interior and exterior of the property, gather data on recent sales of competitive properties, and apply the sales comparison approach.	Do it! Develop that opinion of market value.
The client, a lender, is considering making a relatively small, low-risk loan to a borrower with good credit.	Is the property adequate security for the loan?	Inspect the exterior only (drive-by), collect and analyze sale data, and apply the sales comparison approach.	Do it! Develop an opinion of market value.
The client is representing a party in a lawsuit over construction defects in an office building.	How much loss in value, if any, do the defects cause?	Inspect the interior and exterior of the property; obtain information from engineer on the nature and extent of damage and cost to cure, gather data on recent sales of competitive properties, construction costs, rents, operating expenses; apply the sales comparison, cost, and income approaches.	Do it! Develop an opinion of market value.

In appraisal practice, what are the ramifications of failing to properly identify the client's problem to be solved? Consider what's going wrong in the following examples.

Example 1

The owner of a small, single-tenant office building requests an appraisal to assist him in deciding whether to dispose of the property or refinance it. The property is known to contain asbestos, and the appraiser is made aware of this. However, the appraiser completes the appraisal on the basis of a hypothetical condition that the property contains no asbestos or other hazardous substances. Upon reading the appraisal report, the client becomes upset because he wanted to know the value taking the asbestos into account.

Example 2

A property owner engages an appraiser to appraise his property but does not tell the appraiser why he needs the appraisal (the intended use), and the appraiser does not inquire. The appraiser completes the appraisal assignment and delivers a report to the property owner, who then takes it to a lender to support an application for a loan. The lender refuses to accept the appraisal, citing the appraisal requirements pursuant to the Federal Financial Instutions Reform, Recovery and Enforcement Act (FIRREA), which prohibit borrower-engaged appraisals. The property owner is furious, believing he was deceived by the appraiser.

Example 3

An appraiser is hired by a corporation's CFO to provide an appraisal "for internal purposes." Three weeks after delivering the completed report, the client contacts the appraiser and asks him to sign a copy of Form 8283, which is required by the IRS in connection with a charitable donation. By signing the form, the appraiser attests to the following: "I am qualified to make appraisals of the type of property being valued...I understand that a false or fraudulent overstatement of the property value as described in the qualified appraisal or this appraisal summary may subject me to the penalty under section 6701(a) (aiding and abetting the understatement of tax liability)..." The appraiser reviews this form and is concerned about whether his report contains sufficient information for IRS tax-reporting purposes.

In each of the foregoing cases, the problem to be solved and appraiser's solution (scope of work) are mismatched. The result is a disappointed client, a misled client, and/or an appraiser who now finds he has gone out on a limb in terms of responsibility and liability.

If the appraiser does understand the problem to be solved, he or she might provide a very good solution–but to the wrong problem! A client who recognizes the mismatch will be understandably upset. Worse, a client who does not recognize the mismatch will likely be misled.

We'll talk in depth about Step 1, identification of the problem to be solved, in Chapter 5. In Chapter 6 we'll address Step 2, planning the solution (or scope of work.) In appraisal practice, Step 3 involves the actual application of the appraisal process (or appraisal review process or appraisal consulting process), a subject that is not covered here. For more information on applying the appraisal process, there are numerous other appraisal texts and courses.

First, in Chapter 2, we will provide some background about the origins and evolution of the scope of work concept.

Origin and Evolution of Scope of Work

A relatively new concept, scope of work, was introduced into USPAP in 1999. Before, the appraisal development process was varied only by being complete or limited, depending on whether the appraiser invoked the Departure Rule. An appraisal either met all the development requirements of USPAP, or it did not. Under this top-down approach, the ideal, or at least superior, appraisal process was the one with the most analysis. An appraisal that included less analysis was, by definition, less reliable, and therefore, sometimes perceived as inferior.

Scope of work is a more evolved concept than departure. Following the scope of work principle, the appraiser first identifies the client, the intended user(s), the intended use of the assignment results, and the type of value to be developed. Then, using this information, the appraiser tailors the amount of research and analysis to the assignment. Thus, for every assignment, there is an ideal solution. Rather than follow a standardized procedure for every assignment, the appraiser must consider the best solution for the problem at hand.

The difference between scope of work and departure can be illustrated mathematically, in the following tables:

Table 2.1: Departure Rule	
Complete Appraisal	All standards rules applied, regardless of whether or not they are necessary
Minus	
Specific Requirements	Specific Requirements = standards rules from which departure is permitted.
Equals	
Limited Appraisal	Limited appraisal inherently less reliable than complete appraisal

Table 2.2: Scope of Work	
Application of standards rules that are always critical, to any assignment	Critical rules include ethics and competency requirements, identification of problem to be solved, and identification of appropriate scope of work
Plus	
Standards rules that are necessary to the assignment at hand	Applicable standards rules vary, depending on the circumstances
Equals	
Ideal solution set for this assignment	Customized solution that leads to credible results, given the intended use

How did the scope of work concept evolve? What were the circumstances that led to this change? Let's go back in history to find out.

Before 1989, appraisers typically had a limited number of tools in their toolboxes when it came to providing appraisal services. They approached every valuation problem using, more or less, the same methodology. Regardless of the reason the client needed the value opinion, they applied the same level of diligence (and faulted each other if "less" was done). They offered their clients four general categories of appraisal reports:

- Full narrative reports
- Executive summary reports
- Letters of opinion
- Form reports

Full narrative reports were commonly used for commercial/industrial property appraisals when the client needed–for whatever reason– a significant amount of detail. Executive summary reports were also commonly used for commercial and industrial appraisals, but were prepared when the client needed only a summary of the information. Letters of opinion were used when the client didn't want any detail, but did want the appraiser's opinion in writing. Form reports were used almost exclusively for one- to four-family residential appraisals as well as for some commercial and industrial appraisals.

These industry-recognized, standard products dictated not only the amount of information provided in the report, but the level and degree of research and analysis that went with the process of developing the value opinion (what we now refer to as "scope of work"). Their preparation encompassed the development and reporting processes together. Neither appraisers nor their clients gave much thought, if any, to the separation of the two. Thus, a shorter report generally indicated that the amount of research and analysis undertaken by the appraiser was similarly brief.

When it was first written in 1987, USPAP did not mention any specific report form or format. An appraisal report was required by USPAP to address the information considered; the appraisal procedures followed, as did the reasoning that supported the analyses, opinions and conclusions. There was no clear direction as to the level of detail required. However, at that time, the Departure Provision could be applied to certain reporting requirements, and this suggested that some flexibility might be possible in the reporting process as well as in the development process.

The appraisal regulations pursuant to FIRREA that were adopted by the bank regulatory agencies initially prohibited the use of the Departure Provision in appraisals for federally related transactions (FRTs). Thus, it seemed that, for lenders at least, only one type of appraisal report was permitted for commercial and industrial properties (a full narrative) and one type for residential properties (the URAR form.) It didn't take long for this one-size-fits-all approach to prove itself to be unworkable. In the commercial/industrial arena, lenders found themselves presented with weighty tomes that seemed to be overkill, given the nature of the transaction at hand. Similarly, in the residential arena, a URAR report with a walk-through or interior inspection of the improvements seemed unnecessary when the borrower was applying for a relatively small, low-risk loan.

Lending clients wanted something different. But appraisers felt their hands were tied by USPAP requirements. It seemed that "less" should be allowable in some cases.

Facing mounting concerns about this situation, the ASB made significant revisions to USPAP in 1994. It recognized that there were two related issues at stake: flexibility in the process of developing an opinion of value and flexibility in the amount of information that must be reported. As a result, the ASB adopted Statement on Appraisal Standards No. 7 (SMT-7), which clarified the applicability of the departure provision (subsequently renamed the departure rule) in the appraisal development process. (It is interesting to note that this was not a change per se; the departure provision had existed all along and could be applied to the development process.) The Board also revised Standard 2 to permit three different reporting options for written appraisal reports, thereby allowing for some degree of flexibility in the reporting process.

The terms *complete appraisal* and *limited appraisal* were introduced into USPAP to distinguish between an appraisal in which the departure provision was not invoked and one in which the departure provision was invoked. The terms *self-contained appraisal report, summary appraisal report,* and *restricted use appraisal report* were given to the three written report options. The three report options, together with the two types of appraisals, resulted in six possible development/reporting combinations:

Development	Reporting
Complete Appraisal	Self-Contained Appraisal Report
Complete Appraisal	Summary Appraisal Report
Complete Appraisal	Restricted Use Appraisal Report
Limited Appraisal	Self-Contained Appraisal Report
Limited Appraisal	Summary Appraisal Report
Limited Appraisal	Restricted Use Appraisal Report

In addition, a complete or limited appraisal could be reported orally (verbally)

Note: The same options were available for real property appraisal, personal property appraisal, and business appraisal, as reflected in Standards 1 and 2, 7 and 8, and 9 and 10, respectively. Subsequently, however, Standard 10 was modified, so that there were two reporting options for written business appraisals.

Despite this attempt to allow flexibility in USPAP, the departure rule has proven to be confusing to appraisers as well as to their clients. While USPAP does not require the appraiser to state in the report whether the appraisal process was complete or limited, USPAP does require the appraiser to discuss any departures. Unfortunately, many appraisal reports have included the label "limited," yet failed to explain the departures invoked.

Further, while USPAP has always been very clear that the burden of proof is on the appraiser to make the decision to depart, many appraisers have simply followed a client's direction to depart without considering the appropriateness of doing so under the specific circumstances.

Clients for appraisal services have often misunderstood the application of the Departure Rule and the three reporting options. To some clients—and to some appraisers—"limited appraisal" became code words for "less expensive," without concern for the risk taken in relying on that appraisal for a certain use. To others, a "limited appraisal" meant an abridged version that lacks substance. To still others, it is incomprehensible why an appraisal process that excludes an interior property inspection but includes all three of the typical approaches to value is called a "complete appraisal," yet one that includes an interior inspection but excludes an approach to value is called a "limited appraisal."

By the late 1990s the ASB recognized that the departure concept was not working as well as it had hoped. It was not providing the needed flexibility in a clear, understandable, and practical manner. And it was too readily open to abuse. The ASB began to consider ways to improve USPAP by more clearly stating the appraiser's responsibility to first identify the problem to be solved and second to identify the appropriate steps necessary to solve the problem.

In 1999 the scope of work concept was introduced to Standard 1. (It was later introduced to all of the other development standards, including the standards for appraisal review and appraisal consulting.) The words "given the scope of work identified" were added to the Standards Rules that address the data collection and analysis process, allowing modification of the work done by the appraiser.

The ASB also changed their thinking on the concept of reliability. Statement 7, first issued in 1994, said that the level of reliability decreases as the degree of departure increases. The ASB no longer believed this to be true. Changes were made to Statement 7 to reflect the new thinking: "reliability" is relative to the intended use. In other words, an appraisal for which the scope of work is narrowed might be perfectly reliable for one intended use, but not for another. This concept is key to understanding how scope of work functions as a flexibility mechanism in USPAP.

On October 28, 2005, the ASB finalized changes to USPAP, effective July 1, 2006. The changes included elimination of the Departure Rule and the terms "complete" and "limited," and the introduction of a new Scope of Work Rule. At the same time, the ASB introduced two new guidance pieces, Advisory Opinion 28 (AO-28) "Inspection of the Subject Property," and Advisory Opinion 29 (AO-29) "An Acceptable Scope of Work."

Throughout the remainder of this text, any references to USPAP are to the 2006 edition.

Chapter 3

The term *scope* is defined in the *American Heritage® Dictionary of the English Language* as follows:

Scope (skōp)
n.

1. The range of one's perceptions, thoughts, or actions.
2. Breadth or opportunity to function.
3. The area covered by a given activity or subject.
4. The length or sweep of a mooring cable.
5. Informal. A viewing instrument such as a periscope, microscope, or telescope.

[Italian scopo, aim, purpose, from Greek skopos, target, aim. See spek- in Indo-European Roots.[1]]

When the term *scope of work* was first introduced into USPAP in 1999, it was only with regard to Standard 1 (real property appraisal development.) Subsequently, the phrase was inserted into all the other development standards, including Standard 3 (appraisal review) and Standard 4 (appraisal consulting). Now the

> Note that scope of work is now included in Standard 3 (appraisal review), Standard 4 (appraisal consulting), Standard 6 (mass appraisal), Standard 7 (personal property appraisal), and Standard 9 (business and intangible asset appraisal).

---

1. *The American Heritage® Dictionary of the English Language,* 4th ed. (Boston: Houghton Mifflin Company, 2000).

scope of work concept is a thread that runs throughout the USPAP document. In order to better understand how scope functions as a flexibility mechanism, let's closely examine USPAP to see where and how the phrase is used.

Definition

USPAP's definitions section includes the following entry:

SCOPE OF WORK: the type and extent of research and analyses in an assignment.

The Scope of Work Rule elaborates further on this definition:

Comment: Scope of work includes, but is not limited to:

- the extent to which the property is identified;
- the extent to which tangible property is inspected;
- the type and extent of data researched; and
- the type and extent of analyses applied to arrive at opinions or conclusions.

Scope of work encompasses all of the steps taken in the appraisal development process, not only those that are specifically mentioned in USPAP's standards rules. For example, USPAP does not require a property inspection. Instead, it requires that the characteristics of the subject property relevant to the assignment be identified. There are many ways to accomplish this identification process. A visual inspection is one means of obtaining information about the property. But to what degree is the inspection carried out? Will you observe the property from the street only? Will you enter the premises? If you enter the premises, will you visually inspect every room? Will you inspect the basement, or the attic? How about the crawl space? Will you measure the improvements, or obtain their square footage from county records or building plans? Will you go so far as to pull up the carpeting to examine the sub-flooring? Will you open and close every door, window, and drawer to substantiate your opinion of the property's condition? Will you enter and look at each of the 450 units in the subject apartment complex?

Appraisers have been making such decisions all along. In many ways, the scope of work decision is not new. What is new is the degree to which we can apply the concept to other facets of the appraisal process.

Scope of Work Rule

The Scope of Work Rule begins with a discussion of the definition of scope of work. It then reminds us that the appraiser must be prepared to demonstrate that the scope of work is sufficient to produce credible assignment results, that credible assignment results require support by relevant evidence and logic, and that the credibility of assignment results is always measured in the context of the intended use. Following this introductory section, the Scope of Work Rule contains three subsections:

- Problem Identification
- Scope of Work Acceptability
- Disclosure Obligations

These topics will be addressed at length in Chapters 5, 6, and 7.

Scope of Work in the Real Property Appraisal Standards

Let's examine Standards Rule 1, which sets forth the requirements for developing a real property appraisal (but not communicating, or reporting, it.)

The very first line in Standards Rule 1 states:

> In developing a real property appraisal, an appraiser must identify the problem to be solved, determine the scope of work necessary to solve the problem, and correctly complete research and analyses necessary to produce a credible appraisal.

This one line succinctly summarizes the three steps to solving the appraisal problem:

1. Identify the problem.
2. Plan the solution.
3. Apply the solution.

Note also how the goal of the appraisal process is a "credible appraisal." We will talk more on this point in the next chapter.

The phrase "scope of work" is found next in Standards Rule 1-2(h).

This standards rule states the firm requirement, applicable to every appraisal assignment, to determine the scope of work for the assignment. Remember, Standards Rule 1 is a development standard so essentially the requirement to determine means to think it up or figure it out. However, this requirement, like many of the requirements in Standards Rule 1, becomes a reporting requirement in Standards Rule 2.

Let's take a quick look at where scope of work is found in Standards Rule 2. For any written appraisal report, the scope of work that was used to develop the appraisal must be discussed. The only difference between the three reporting options is the level of detail required with regard to that discussion. A self-contained appraisal report is detailed throughout, so the requirement is to present the scope discussion with a good deal of detail. A summary appraisal report contains summarized information; that is, it presents all of the relevant information in a brief, succinct manner. A restricted use appraisal report does not contain much detail, so the requirement regarding the scope discussion is merely to state it.

In an oral report, the appraiser must make an effort to verbally present as much information as would be presented in a summary appraisal report, though that is not always practical. However, the scope of work is such an important part of the report that it requires as much attention as possible in oral-reporting situations.

Scope of Work in Standard 3—Appraisal Review, Development, and Reporting

The first sentence in Standards Rule 3 underscores the importance of scope of work in the process of developing an appraisal review opinion and the importance of disclosing the scope of work in the appraisal review report:

> In performing an appraisal review assignment, an appraiser acting as a reviewer must develop and report a credible opinion as to the quality of another appraiser's work and must clearly disclose the scope of work performed.

The requirement to determine the scope of work appropriate for the assignment is addressed in Standards Rule 3-1(c).

> Standards Rule 3-1(c)
>
> In developing an appraisal review, the reviewer must determine the scope of work necessary to produce credible assignment results in accordance with the SCOPE OF WORK RULE.

The reviewer's scope of work should not be confused with the appraiser's scope of work. The reviewer's scope of work is the problem-solving process of the reviewer, or what the reviewer would do to answer the question about the quality of the work done by the appraiser. In the appraisal review process there are myriad ways to adjust the scope of work. For example, the reviewer's scope might be limited to simply checking the math in the work under review. Or, it might include the development of the reviewer's own opinion of value. If the reviewer develops his or her own opinion of value, the scope involved may or may not include additional research into market data, an inspection of the subject property, or a reanalysis of highest and best use, or not.

We then find the phrase "scope of work" in Standards Rules 3-1(d), (e), (f), and (g).

> Standards Rule 3-1(d)
>
> In developing an appraisal review, the reviewer must develop an opinion as to the completeness of the material under review, given the reviewer's scope of work

The degree to which Standards Rules 3-1(d), (e), (f) and (g) are applicable depends entirely on the reviewer's scope of work. For example, the reviewer's scope might (or might not) include an independent search for market data and analysis of that data. The applicability of Standards Rules 3-1(d), (e), (f) and (g) will also depend on what is being reviewed. Clearly, if the subject of the review is only a portion of an appraisal report, the reviewer will develop these opinions with regard to just that portion.

The requirement for reporting the results of an appraisal review is addressed in Standards Rule 3-2. Standards Rule 3-2(c) addresses disclosure of the scope of work:

Standards Rule 3-2(d) requires the reviewer to report his or her findings with regard to the quality of the work under review, given the reviewer's scope as identified.

Scope of Work in the Real Property Appraisal Consulting Standards

The lead-in sentence to the development standard for real property appraisal consulting addresses the three steps to problem solving, and is identical to the first sentence to Standards Rule 1.

Likewise, Standards Rule 4-2(h) is identical to Standards Rule 1-2(h), requiring the determination of the correct scope of work for the assignment. It should be noted, however, that the comment to this standards rule is lengthy and contains much information about the development of the value opinion that is a part of the development of the real property appraisal consulting opinion.

Standards Rule 5–2(f) addresses the requirement for disclosure of the scope of work in a real property appraisal consulting report.

Scope of Work in the Personal Property Appraisal Standards

Standards Rule 7 sets forth the requirements for developing a personal property appraisal, and Standards Rule 8 sets forth the requirements for communicating, or reporting, it. Standards Rules 7 and 8 are very similar to Standards Rules 1 and 2, respectively; especially in the way they address scope of work.

The very first line in Standards Rule 7 states:

> In developing a real property appraisal, an appraiser must identify the problem to be solved, determine the scope of work necessary to solve the problem, and correctly complete research and analyses necessary to produce a credible appraisal.

This one line is a quick summary of the three steps to solving the appraisal problem–the three steps that were the topic of discussion in Chapter 1 (identify the problem, plan the solution, and apply the solution.) Note that this same statement is found at the beginning of the real property and business appraisal development standards (Standards Rules 1 and 9.)

We find the phrase "scope of work" addressed directly in Standards Rule 7-2(h), which is identical to Standards Rule 1-2(h) and 9-2(h).

> Standards Rule 7-2(h)
>
> An appraiser must determine the scope of work necessary to produce credible assignment results in accordance with the SCOPE OF WORK RULE.

This Standards Rule states the firm requirement, applicable to every assignment, to identify the scope of work for the assignment. Standards Rule 7 is a development standard, so, essentially, the requirement to "identify" means to "think it up." However, this requirement, like many of the requirements in Standards Rule 7, becomes a reporting requirement in Standards Rule 8.

Let's take a quick look at where the requirement to report scope of work is found in Standards Rule 8.

> Standards Rule 8-2(a) vii
>
> The content of a Self-Contained Appraisal Report must describe the scope of work used to develop the appraisal.

For any written appraisal report, the scope of work that was used to develop the appraisal must be discussed. The only difference between the three reporting options is the level of detail required with regard to that discussion.

Note that the requirements for written personal property appraisal reports are essentially identical to the requirements for written real property appraisal reports.

In an oral report, the appraiser must make an effort to verbally present as much information as would be presented in a summary appraisal report, though that is not always practical. However, the scope of work is such an important part of the report that it requires as much attention as possible in oral reporting situations.

Scope of Work in the Business Appraisal Standards

The business appraisal standards are very similar to the real property and personal property appraisal standards. A key difference is that the business property appraisal-reporting standard includes two, not three, written reporting options.

Let's examine Standards Rule 9, which sets forth the requirements for developing a business appraisal (but not communicating, or reporting, it.)

The very first line in Standards Rule 9 states:

Note also that this same statement is found at the beginning of the real property and personal property appraisal development standards

(Standards Rules 1 and 7) This one line is a quick summary of the three steps to solving the appraisal problem–the three steps that were the topic of discussion in Chapter 1 (identify the problem, plan the solution, apply the solution.) Note how the goal of the appraisal process is a *credible appraisal.* We will talk more on this point in the next chapter.

We find the phrase "scope of work" addressed directly in Standards Rule 9-2(h), which is identical to Standards Rule 1-2(h) and 7-2(h).

This Standards Rule states the firm requirement, applicable to every assignment, to identify the scope of work for the assignment. Standards Rule 9 is a development standard, so, essentially, the requirement to "identify" means to "think it up." However, this requirement, like many of the requirements in Standard 9, becomes a reporting requirement in Standards Rule 10.

Let's take a quick look at where the requirement to report "scope of work" is found in Standards Rule 10.

The standards rules that address written business appraisal reports are virtually identical to those for written real property appraisal and personal property appraisal reports, except that there is essentially no separate set of requirements for a self-contained format. (The appraisal report in Standard 10 is like a summary appraisal report in Standards 2 and 8.) For any written appraisal report, the scope of work that was used to develop the appraisal must be discussed. The only difference between the two reporting options is the level of detail required with regard to that discussion.

In an oral business appraisal report, the appraiser must make an effort to verbally present as much information as would be presented in an appraisal report, though that is not always practical. However, the scope of work is such an important part of the report that it requires as much attention as possible in oral reporting situations.

Chapter 4

The first sentence in USPAP's appraisal and appraisal consulting development standards (Standards Rules 1, 4, 7, and 9) states that an appraiser "must identify the problem to be solved, determine the scope of work necessary to solve the problem, and correctly complete the research and analyses necessary to produce credible results." The objective is always a credible result. Not "the right number." Not "an irrefutable conclusion."

The term *credible* is a key concept in USPAP. A definition of credible was added with the 2006 edition. *Credible* means worthy of belief. The definition's apparent simplicity disguises its true complexity. Worthy of belief by whom? The definition doesn't specify. It's open ended, which means, essentially, that it must be credible to the public. Whereas USPAP's requirement for reporting (stated in Standards Rule 2-1(b)) is that the report must be understandable to the intended users, USPAP requires that the assignment results be credible to any and all who may be in a position to judge.

The comment to the definition states that "credible assignment results require support, by relevant evidence and logic, to the degree necessary for the intended use." Thus, credibility relates directly to–and is measured in light of–intended use. The objective of any assignment can be restated, then, as a credible opinion that is useful in solving the client's problem.

Reliability is a related, but quite different, concept. It is the ability of the intended user to rely on the assignment results. Reliability is also relative to the intended use of the assignment. The results of an assignment could be reliable for one intended use, but not for another.

Accuracy is the correctness of the data and analysis applied. An appraisal must always be accurate. Reducing the scope of work applied never gives the appraiser license to be inaccurate. Whatever the degree of data and analysis applied, it must be factually and technically correct.

Given that the goal is to be credible, the scope of work necessary to attain such credibility may be adjusted, or varied, depending on the assignment. Where in USPAP does this become clear? Let's look at the Standards Rules that address credibility.

The very first sentence in Standards Rules 1, 3, 4, 6, 7, and 9 (all of the development standards) stress that the goal of any assignment is credible results. Standards Rule 1 reads as follows, but note that the wording to the other development standards is either identical or very similar:

> In developing a real property appraisal, an appraiser must identify the problem to be solved, determine the scope of work necessary to solve the problem, and correctly complete research and analyses necessary to produce a credible appraisal.

The concept of credibility continues to be stressed in the first standards rule, Standards Rule 1-1(a). Again, here it is for real property appraisal, but note that Standards Rules 4-1(a), 7-1(a), and 9-1(a) for appraisal consulting, personal property appraisal, and business appraisal are virtually identical.

> Standards Rule 1-1
>
> In developing a real property appraisal, an appraiser must:
>
> (a) be aware of, understand, and correctly employ those recognized methods and techniques that are necessary to produce a credible appraisal;

Standards Rule 1-1(a) is essentially an extension of the competency rule. The appraiser must be competent enough to understand what needs to be done to solve the problem and must be competent with regard to recognized methods and techniques. What are recognized methods and techniques? One must consider what the appraiser's peers would do in a similar situation to answer that question. This concept is discussed in more detail in Chapter 6. The goal, always, is a credible appraisal.

Standards Rules 1-2(f) and (g) address the use of extraordinary assumptions and hypothetical conditions. Again, virtually the same wording is found in Standards Rules 4-1(f) and (g), 7-1(f) and (g), and 9-1(f) and (g) for appraisal consulting, personal property appraisal, and business appraisal.

These two standards rules read identically, but Standards Rule 1-2(f) deals with extraordinary assumptions while Standards Rule 1-2(g) deals with hypothetical conditions. Misuse of either of these can cause an appraisal to be not credible for the intended use.

Standards Rule 1-2(h) sets forth the requirement for determining the scope of work, and links the appropriateness of the scope determination directly to credibility. Again, virtually the same wording is found in Standards Rules 4-2(h), 7-2(h), and 9-2(h) for appraisal consulting, personal property appraisal, and business appraisal.

Standards Rule 1-2(h) succinctly states the second step in the problem-solving process. Quite simply, it says the appraiser must figure out how to solve the problem. What is the plan of attack? What needs to be done in order to produce credible results?

This standards rule is a "must" requirement, there are absolutely no exceptions. USPAP recognizes that whenever an opinion of value is developed by an appraiser, identifying the scope of work is one of the key steps. Note that this Standards Rule is a development requirement, though there is a corresponding reporting requirement in Standard 2.

Standards Rule 1-3 addresses the need to develop a highest and best use opinion in a market value assignment. Similar wording can be found in Standards Rule 7-3 for personal property appraisal:

Standards Rule 1-3 applies only when the type of value (purpose) is market value. If the assignment is to develop another type of opinion, such as use value or investment value, Standards Rule 1-3 doesn't apply at all. For market value appraisals, this standards rule requires the appraiser to identify and analyze land use regulations, supply and demand, physical adaptability of the real estate, and market area trends.

It also requires the appraiser to develop an opinion of the highest and best use of the real estate. These issues are always critical—to some degree—to the development of a market value opinion. Highest and best use, for one, dictates just what the subject property consists of, i.e, what is the property in the eyes of the market? For example, a single-family residence located on land zoned for commercial use surrounded by commercial properties in an area with growing demand for commercial space might be viewed by the market–the group of most probable buyers–as a commercial site, not a single-family residence.

While the appraiser must always give some consideration to such issues, USPAP recognizes that the level of work applied can vary. For instance, highest and best use analysis for some assignments might involve a thorough feasibility study (e.g., a proposed regional shopping mall in an appraisal for construction loan purposes.) For others, the development of a highest and best use opinion can adequately be completed in a matter of seconds (e.g., a tract home in the middle of a large development of similar tract homes, again for loan purposes.) Thus, the appraiser must do what is necessary as far as highest and best use analysis is concerned to develop credible assignment results.

Standards Rules 1-4 (a) through (c) address the application of the three approaches, while Standards Rules 1-4 (d) through (g) address assorted issues that, if they pertain to the assignment, must be addressed. The wording in Standards Rule 7-4 for personal property appraisal is almost identical, and it is similar in Standards Rule 9-4 for business appraisal.

Standards Rule 1-4

In developing a real property appraisal, an appraiser must collect, verify, and analyze all information necessary for credible assignment results.

(a) When a sales comparison approach is necessary for credible assignment results, an appraiser must analyze such comparable sales data as are available to indicate a value conclusion.

(b) When a cost approach is necessary for credible assignment results, an appraiser must:

  (i)   develop an opinion of site value by an appropriate appraisal method or technique;

  (ii) analyze such comparable cost data as are available to estimate the cost new of the improvements (if any); and

  (iii) analyze such comparable data as are available to estimate the difference between the cost new and the present worth of the improvements (accrued depreciation).

(c) When an income approach is necessary to get credible assignment results, an appraiser must:

  (i)   analyze such comparable rental data as are available and/or the potential earnings capacity of the property to estimate the gross income potential of the property;

(ii)   analyze such comparable operating expense data as are available to estimate the operating expenses of the property;

(iii) analyze such comparable data as are available to estimate rates of capitalization and/or rates of discount; and

(iv)   base projections of future rent and/or income potential and expenses on reasonably clear and appropriate evidence.

> Comment: In developing income and expense statements and cash flow projections, an appraiser must weigh historical information and trends, current supply and demand factors affecting such trends, and anticipated events such as competition from developments under construction.

(d) When developing an opinion of the value of a leased fee estate or a leasehold estate, an appraiser must analyze the effect on value, if any, of the terms and conditions of the lease(s).

(e) When analyzing the assemblage of the various estates or component parts of a property, an appraiser must analyze the effect on value, if any, of the assemblage. An appraiser must refrain from valuing the whole solely by adding together the individual values of the various estates or component parts.

> Comment: Although the value of the whole may be equal to the sum of the separate estates or parts, it also may be greater than or less than the sum of such estates or parts. Therefore, the value of the whole must be tested by reference to appropriate data and supported by an appropriate analysis of such data.
>
> A similar procedure must be followed when the value of the whole has been established and the appraiser seeks to value a part. The value of any such part must be tested by reference to appropriate data and supported by an appropriate analysis of such data.

(f) When analyzing anticipated public or private improvements, located on or off the site, an appraiser must analyze the effect on value, if any, of such anticipated improvements to the extent they are reflected in market actions.

(g) When personal property, trade fixtures, or intangible items are included in the appraisal, the appraiser must analyze the effect on value of such non-real property items.

> Comment: When the scope of work includes an appraisal of personal property, trade fixtures or intangible items, competency in personal property appraisal (see Standard 7) or business appraisal (see Standard 9) is required.

In the application of the three approaches, the appraiser must do what is necessary in order to develop credible assignment results. There is no requirement to do more than is necessary. If the work is not necessary in order to develop credible results, there is no reason to do it.

When we say "work," we might be referring to an entire approach to value. Or, we could be talking about a step within that approach. An appraiser might determine that an approach to value is not necessary at all. For example, an income approach might not be necessary in the valuation of a single-family residence. Or a cost approach might not be necessary in the valuation of a retail property for which there is an abundance of comparable rental and sales data.

Or, the appraiser might determine that the degree to which the steps within an approach are applied can be tailored to the assignment. For example, for some assignments, in applying the sales comparison approach, it may be adequate to look no further than one's own appraisal files for comparable sales. For other assignments, it may be necessary to search county records. In analyzing sales in the sales comparison approach, for some assignments it may be adequate to merely examine the unadjusted price range. For other assignments, adjustments to those sales using paired sales analysis may be necessary.

As we can see, there is now a great deal of flexibility allowed in USPAP in the appraisal, appraisal review, and appraisal consulting development process. In the next chapter, we will examine the nature of an assignment and how the scope of work decision relates to the assignment's parameters.

Chapter 5

Problem Identification: The Significant Seven

As we discussed in Chapter 1, the first of the three steps to solving a problem is to identify the problem. You cannot derive a solution–let alone figure out how to go about deriving one–until you know exactly what the problem is. Thus, every assignment must begin with a clear understanding regarding the following seven parameters–the significant seven: client, intended users, intended use, type of opinion, effective date, relevant characteristics about the subject of the assignment, and assignment conditions.

This may sound simplistic, but this crucial first step is often given too little attention, or overlooked altogether. Many faulty appraisals start out badly, with the failure on the part of the appraiser to truly understand the problem to be solved. Many of the misunderstandings between appraisers and their clients about appraisals are caused by this failure.

The good news is that the remedy is easy. It requires the appraiser to do what nearly all professionals in any field must do: Begin with a consultation process with the client to uncover certain key pieces of information. Once adequately informed, the appraiser can delineate the problem to be solved and then plan the solution.

USPAP's Scope of Work Rule clearly sets forth the requirement to identify the problem to be solved. It is applicable to any assignment (appraisal, appraisal review, or appraisal consulting) and any property type (real property, personal property, or business property.)

Within the Scope of Work Rule there is a section on problem identification:

Problem Identification

An appraiser must gather and analyze information about those assignment elements that are necessary to properly identify the appraisal, appraisal review or appraisal-consulting problem to be solved.

Comment: The assignment elements necessary for problem identification are addressed in the applicable Standards Rules (i.e., SR 1-2, SR 3-1, SR 4-2, SR 6-2, SR 7-2 and SR 9-2). In an appraisal assignment, for example, identification of the problem to be solved requires the appraiser to identify the following assignment elements:

- client and any other intended users;
- intended use of the appraiser's opinions and conclusions;
- type and definition of value;
- effective date of the appraiser's opinions and conclusions;
- subject of the assignment and its relevant characteristics; and
- assignment conditions.

This information provides the appraiser with the basis for determining the type and extent of research and analyses to include in the development of an appraisal. Similar information is necessary for problem identification in appraisal review and appraisal consulting assignments.

Communication with the client is required to establish most of the information necessary for problem identification. However, the identification of relevant characteristics is a judgment made by the appraiser that requires competency in that type of assignment.

> Assignment conditions include assumptions, extraordinary assumptions, hypothetical conditions, supplemental standards, jurisdictional exceptions, and other conditions that affect the scope of work.

We'll examine these requirements closely in the pages that follow. First, however, we must ensure a good understanding of a key term: assignment. The introduction of this term into appraisal practice heralded a new milestone in the evolution of the profession, and it's important to know why.

Assignment

When scope of work was introduced to USPAP in 1999, the definition of the term *assignment* was also added. USPAP's definition section includes the following entry:

> ASSIGNMENT: a valuation service provided as a consequence of an agreement between an appraiser and a client.

The new emphasis on the assignment signaled a major change in focus. Thinking in terms of assignments rather than appraisal reports alters the mind-set of both appraisers and their clients about the nature of the service that appraisers provide. Appraisers do not sell appraisal reports. Rather, they sell their expertly developed opinions—or, more specifically, the right for a particular intended user to rely on their expertly developed opinion.

The goal of an appraisal assignment is a credible opinion of value—not the production of an appraisal report. An appraisal report is merely the means by which the results of an assignment are communicated to the client and intended users. An assignment involves a relationship between an appraiser and a client—a relationship that carries with it significant ramifications regarding trust, confidentiality, disclosure, and liability.

Implied in the definition of assignment is the need for a meeting of the minds between the appraiser and the client as to the parameters for the service to be provided.

The Significant Seven

1. Client. Who is hiring you?
2. Intended user. Who intends to use the appraisal?
3. Intended use. Why are they going to rely on it?
4. Type of opinion.
5. Effective date of opinion.
6. Relevant characteristics about the subject of the assignment.
7. Assignment conditions.

These seven parameters identify the problem to be solved. They must be known in order for the appraiser to figure out how to proceed. That is, they must be known to decide the appropriate scope of work.

An appraiser must refuse an assignment in which one or more of these parameters is not known, or if the client will not reveal enough information for them to be known.

Also, if any one of these seven parameters changes once the assignment is begun, the appraiser and client need to go back to the drawing board on the assignment, and re-establish a meeting of the minds with regard to it. In effect, the assignment becomes a new assignment– a "do-over." Why? Because the scope of work could be impacted.

For example, if the client informs the appraiser after the appraisal process is begun that a more current effective date of value is needed, the appraiser must consider how that revised date of value might alter the nature of the appraisal development process–i.e., the scope of work. In another example, if the client informs the appraiser of an additional intended user, the appraiser must consider whether the scope of work, as well as the manner in which the assignment results are communicated (reporting process) must be adjusted.

Scope of work allows an appraiser to customize an assignment to meet the needs of the client. It's important to recognize how a client's needs and wants can differ. For example, a lender needs an appraisal that complies with federal regulations and USPAP. But the lender wants to close the loan.

To properly identify the client's needs, the appraiser must consult with the client at the beginning of an assignment to properly identify them. USPAP requires the appraiser to have a clear understanding of the client's intended use, as well as the six other key assignment parameters, in order to structure the assignment properly.

Let's look more closely at each of the seven assignment parameters as defined by USPAP.

Client

CLIENT: the party or parties who engage an appraiser (by employment or contract) in a specific assignment.

Comment: The client identified by the appraiser in an appraisal, appraisal review, or appraisal consulting assignment (or in the assignment work file) is the party or parties with whom the appraiser has an appraiser-client relationship in the related assignment, and may be an individual, group, or entity.

The client is, quite simply, the party who is engaging the appraiser. The client could be one person (e.g., Mr. John Doe), or one entity (ABC

Bank). Or, it could be a number of people, or entities, acting together as one for the purpose of hiring the appraiser. As far as USPAP is concerned, it makes no difference whether the appraiser is compensated by the client or by another party. For example, a lender might hire an appraiser, but the borrower might pay the appraiser. This does not make the borrower the client.

Why is it so important to identify the client clearly? From a business practice standpoint, the client is the primary contact person. The client is the one from whom you obtain all your information about the assignment (the rest of the significant seven.) From a USPAP standpoint, the client is the one to whom confidentiality is owed.

Intended Users

> INTENDED USER: the client and any other party as identified, by name or type, as users of the appraisal, appraisal review, or appraisal consulting report by the appraiser on the basis of communication with the client at the time of the assignment.

Intended users are those who the appraiser intends to use the appraisal (or appraisal review, or appraisal consulting assignment.) That is, you, the appraiser, acknowledge that you are developing your expert opinion for their use. Although the client provides you with information about the parties who may be intended users, ultimately it is the appraiser who decides who they are. Why is it so important to identify the intended users? Because your primary responsibility regarding the use of your opinions and conclusions is to them. Further, intended users are those parties to whom the appraiser is responsible for communicating his or her finding in a clear and understandable manner. They are your audience.

It's important to understand that parties who receive, or who might receive, a copy of the report are not automatically intended users. A party becomes an intended user only because the appraiser intends that party to use the report. For further information, see Statement on Appraisal Standards No. 9.

Intended Use

> INTENDED USE: the use or uses of an appraiser's reported appraisal, appraisal review, or appraisal consulting assignment opinions and conclusions, as identified by the appraiser based on communication with the client at the time of the assignment.

Intended use is the appraiser's understanding of why the client and intended users need the service. It is the use (or uses) to which you, the appraiser, intend your opinions and conclusions to be put. Some possible intended uses relate to:

- Financing
- Litigation
- Condemnation
- Divorce settlement
- Buy/Sell decision
- Tax reporting
- Portfolio evaluation
- Arbitration
- Partnership value
- Estate value
- Charitable donation
- Valuation for financial reporting purposes (market-to-market)
- Other

As we'll discuss in the next chapter, intended use is the most important of the significant seven in determining the appropriate scope of work. It is the key driver in making that decision.

Appraisers have not traditionally been in the habit of asking a client why? when requested to provide an appraisal. Yet this is a most important question, for without understanding the client's intended use, the appraiser cannot begin to make the appropriate scope of work decision.

Type of Opinion

The results of an assignment might be an appraisal opinion, appraisal review opinion, appraisal consulting opinion, or some other type of opinion.

In an appraisal assignment, the opinion is some type of value. The type of value is important to identify because there are many different types of value. Some include market value, investment value, and use value, but there are others as well. There are many different definitions of market value in use, and it is important for the appraiser and client to know at the outset which ones will apply. Keep in mind that the appraiser does not decide which type of value will apply; he or she merely identifies the type needed, given the nature of the client's problem.

In an appraisal review assignment, the type of opinion is an opinion about the quality of the work under review.

In an appraisal consulting assignment, the type of opinion may be one of a broad variety of analyses, recommendations, or conclusions. While the objective in an appraisal consulting assignment is never value, arriving at the assignment results always involves value.

Effective Date

The effective date is important because the appraiser's conclusions are reflected as of that date, and that date alone. The effective date can be a current date, a prospective (future) date, or a retrospective (historical) date. Again, the effective date is not decided by the appraiser; it is determined by the nature of the client's problem.

Relevant Characteristics About the Subject of the Assignment

The subject of an appraisal assignment is some type of property–real property, personal property, or business property. The subject of an appraisal review assignment is work done by another appraiser (his or her appraisal, appraisal review or appraisal consulting report, work file, or part thereof.)

In an appraisal assignment, identifying the relevant characteristics means addressing the questions, "What is the subject property?" and "What is its nature?" Keep in mind that in valuing real property, appraisers do not appraise land and improvements; rather, the subject property always consists of interests in land and buildings. So the primary question is, what real property interest is to be appraised? Some possible interests include: fee simple, leased fee, leasehold, easement, or partial interest. Most often it is best to describe the interest appraised, however, rather than to simply give it a label, as these terms may be defined differently by different users.

The nature of the real estate (land and improvements) is important because the value of the interest in the real estate depends on the utility the real estate provides. So it is important to identify, along with the interest appraised, the relevant characteristics of the real estate. Relevance in this instance means to the assignment at hand.

Typically, the primary means of identifying the relevant property characteristics–or at least a significant first step–is to inspect the subject real estate to some degree. In fact, in an appraisal assignment, the sole reason for doing a property inspection is to obtain this information. Contrary to the beliefs of many–including some appraisers–the property inspection serves no other purpose. It is not intended to be a means to uncover and disclose structural defects or needed repairs, except to the degree that such conditions impact value.

When no property inspection is performed (as in the case of a "desktop appraisal"), or only a limited inspection is performed (as in the case of a "drive-by"), then the appraiser must either (1) obtain information about the property characteristics that are relevant to the assignment from other sources, or (2) make assumptions about what those characteristics might be. In either of these two cases, the appraisal would be made based on the extraordinary assumption that the information applied is indeed accurate. Such an extraordinary assumption would have to be prominently disclosed in any appraisal report.

In an appraisal review assignment, the subject is another appraiser's work. Identifying the relevant characteristics means identifying which work. An appraisal report? Part of an appraisal report? A workfile? Some combination of report and workfile?

The subject of an appraisal review could also be another appraiser's appraisal review. Or his appraisal review of an appraisal review.

If the subject of your appraisal review is some type of report, you need to adequately identify it. That is, who prepared it? As of what date? What was the subject of the report?

Assignment Conditions

Assignment conditions include extraordinary assumptions, hypothetical conditions, supplemental standards, and jurisdictional exceptions. Again, the appraiser does not *choose* to apply these in any assignment. Rather, the need for them is driven by the nature of the problem to be solved.

Let's examine each of these four, starting with the respective USPAP definition.

EXTRAORDINARY ASSUMPTION: an assumption, directly related to a specific assignment, which, if found to be false, could alter the appraiser's opinions or conclusions.

Comment: Extraordinary assumptions presume as fact otherwise uncertain information about physical, legal, or economic characteristics of the subject property; or about conditions external to the property, such as market conditions or trends; or about the integrity of data used in an analysis.

Extraordinary assumptions are sometimes necessary in an assignment because of unknowns. To go forward with the assignment, the appraiser must presume something to be true that might not be. And if it isn't true, the opinions or conclusions would likely be different. For example, in the case of a "drive-by" real property appraisal, where the appraiser doesn't do an on-site visit to the property to examine its features, the appraiser must make assumptions in the valuation process about those features (such as size and condition.) These assumptions would be extraordinary assumptions because, if false, the value could be significantly impacted.

Another example of an extraordinary assumption would involve appraising proposed construction. If the date of value is a prospective (future) date when the construction is expected to be complete as proposed, an extraordinary assumption would be that, as of that future date, the construction would indeed be complete as proposed. On the date the appraisal is being prepared, it is unknown whether or not the construction will indeed be complete as of that future date.

Hypothetical conditions are similar to extraordinary assumptions, but they come into play when something that is known to be false is presumed to be true in the appraisal.

HYPOTHETICAL CONDITION: that which is contrary to what exists but is supposed for the purpose of analysis.

Comment: Hypothetical conditions assume conditions contrary to known facts about physical, legal, or economic characteristics of the subject property; or about conditions external to the property, such as market conditions or trends; or about the integrity of data used in an analysis.

An example of the use of a hypothetical condition would involve proposed construction, as in the previous example, but this time, with a current date of value. That is, the property is appraised as though the construction is complete as of today, but as of today, the date of value, it obviously isn't.

Another example would be a property that is known to be contaminated, but the assignment is to value it as though clean. Since it is known that it is contaminated, such an appraisal would be subject to a hypothetical condition that it is not contaminated.

Extraordinary assumptions and hypothetical conditions can be used only when appropriate for the intended use, or, as USPAP says, "if required to develop credible opinions and conclusions," and there is a reasonable basis for using them. Both extraordinary assumptions and hypothetical conditions must be clearly and accurately disclosed in any appraisal report, written or oral.

In the ideal scenario, the need for any extraordinary assumptions or hypothetical conditions would be known at the beginning of the assignment. But the truth of the matter is that many times they aren't known until the appraiser is well into the process of developing the opinions and conclusions. Even so, it's important to try to identify their applicability at the outset when consulting with the client about the assignment.

Supplemental standards may be applicable to an assignment, depending on who the client is and what the intended use is. It's critical to find out about these at the outset of an assignment, not after the fact.

> SUPPLEMENTAL STANDARDS: requirements issued by government agencies, government sponsored enterprises, or other entities that establish public policy which add to the purpose, intent and content of the requirements in USPAP, that have a material effect on the development and reporting of assignment results.
>
> Comment: Supplemental standards are published in regulations, rules, policies, and other similar documents, and have the same applicability to all properties or assignments in a particular category or class regardless of the contracting entity.
>
> Contractual agreements that are unique to the contracting entity and which apply specifically to a particular property or assignment are not supplemental standards.

If your client is a government agency, government-sponsored enterprise, or other entity that establishes public policy, or if your assignment is subject to the requirements of such a body, then supplemental standards may apply. Supplemental standards are simply additional requirements—requirements that go beyond those of USPAP—issued by such an entity.

Be sure to clarify with your client at the outset of the assignment which supplemental standards apply. It is a violation of the Ethics Rule of USPAP to agree to comply with supplemental standards and then to knowingly fail to do so. It is a violation of the Competency Rule of USPAP to agree to comply with supplemental standards and then to inadvertently fail to do so.

Sometimes clients who are not government agencies, government-sponsored enterprises, or other entities that establish public policy have additional requirements regarding an assignment. These are contractual issues between the appraiser and the client. To agree to them and not comply with them may be a breach of contract. As with supplemental standards, the appraiser should clarify with the client at the outset whether there are any such additional requirements.

Jurisdictional exceptions are rarely an issue, but in identifying the problem to be solved, it's important to consider whether or not they will arise.

> JURISDICTIONAL EXCEPTION: an assignment condition that voids the force of a part or parts of USPAP, when compliance with part or parts of USPAP is contrary to law or public policy applicable to the assignment.

Jurisdictional exceptions arise because the assignment is subject to law or public policy, and that law or public policy contradicts a part of USPAP. That is, the law or public policy requires X, but USPAP requires Y, and X and Y are polar opposites. In such a case, the law or public policy effectively trumps USPAP–but only with regard to the conflicting requirement. The rest of USPAP remains intact.

A jurisdictional exception is not invoked by the appraiser. That is, it's not a choice that the appraiser makes, it's a requirement. It is a situation that arises because of a conflict between USPAP and the law or public policy, and it must be dealt with accordingly.

As with supplemental standards, jurisdictional exceptions need to be identified at the beginning of the assignment, not after the fact.

Assignment Planning

Once the seven parameters are addressed, you have essentially identified the problem to be solved. You have set the parameters for the assignment, and are ready to move forward with the next step: Identifying how to solve the problem, otherwise known as the scope of work.

One way to make sure that you've adequately addressed these parameters is to use an assignment plan. An assignment plan is a cheatsheet that you keep handy and fill out during the initial conversation with a potential client about the assignment. An example appears on the following page. The top half of the assignment plan asks for information about the significant seven, while the bottom portion allows you to jot notes about the scope of work. You can then use the assignment plan to prepare an engagement letter, or simply as a guide to help you determine the appropriate scope of work.

Assignment Plan

Client: ____

   Address: _________________   Phone: _______________________

Intended User(s): _______________________________________

Intended Use: ____

Type of Value: ____

Effective Date: ____

Characteristics: ____

   Address: ____

   Legal: ____

   Interest: _________________   Type: _________________________

   Size: _____________________   Age: __________________________

   Lot Size: ____

   Description: ____

Owner's Name: _________________   Phone # ___________________

Extraordinary Assumptions: ______________________________

Hypothetical Conditions: ________________________________

Scope of Work:

   Inspection: ____

   Identify Property:

	❏ Inspection	❏ Appraisal
	❏ Assessor's records	❏ Data bank
	❏ Owner	❏ Buyer
	❏ Agent	❏ State data
	❏ County records	

   Physical Factors: _____________________________________

   Economic Factors: ____________________________________

   Analysis: Type:

	❏ H & B U	❏ Market
	❏ Sales	❏ Cost
	❏ Income	

   Extent: ____

Type of Report: ❏ Self-Contained   ❏ Summary

                ❏ Restricted Use

Date of Completion: _____________   Fee: ________________________

Chapter 6

Scope Determination: What to Do and Why

Once you have identified the problem to be solved, you can move forward with the next step: Planning the solution. In appraisal practice, we refer to planning the solution as determining the scope of work. Just how do you do this? What does USPAP require you to do when it comes to determining the scope of work? And, given that you have many options, what should you do in a specific assignment?

The Scope of Work Rule includes the following section:

SCOPE OF WORK RULE

Scope of Work Acceptability

The scope of work must include the research and analyses that are necessary to develop credible assignment results.

Comment: The scope of work is acceptable when it meets or exceeds:

- the expectations of parties who are regularly intended users for similar assignments; and
- what an appraiser's peers' actions would be in performing the same or a similar assignment.

Determining the scope of work is an ongoing process in an assignment. Information or conditions discovered during the course of an assignment might cause the appraiser to reconsider the scope of work.

An appraiser must be prepared to support the decision to exclude any investigation, information, method, or technique that would appear relevant to the client, another intended user, or the appraiser's peers.

An appraiser must not allow assignment conditions to limit the scope of work to such a degree that the assignment results are not credible in the context of the intended use.

<u>Comment</u>: If relevant information is not available because of assignment conditions that limit research opportunities (such as conditions that place limitations on inspection or information gathering), an appraiser must withdraw from the assignment unless the appraiser can:

- modify the assignment conditions to expand the scope of work to include gathering the information; or
- use an extraordinary assumption about such information, if credible assignment results can still be developed.

An appraiser must not allow the intended use of an assignment or a client's objectives to cause the assignment results to be biased.

The Scope of Work Acceptability section of the Scope of Work Rule provides a quick, two-point test for the appropriateness of the scope decision. That is, the scope of work is acceptable when it meets or exceeds (1) the expectations of parties who are regularly intended users for similar assignments and (2) the actions of one's peers in the same or similar assignment.

Expectations of Intended Users

Intended users are those parties who intend to use your assignment results. Many times, intended users who engage appraisers regularly and have some familiarity with the appraisal process will have their own expectations about what the scope of work should be. For example, lender-clients on single-family residential properties will expect the appraiser to develop a sales comparison approach, but not necessarily a cost approach. Attorney-clients in condemnation cases will likely expect to see before-and-after methodology.

The expectations of informed intended users should suggest to you what an acceptable scope of work will be. Hence, one of the tests in USPAP for the appropriateness of the scope of work decision is the expectations of parties who are regularly intended users for similar assignments.

The Scope of Work Acceptability section of the Scope of Work Rule says that the appraiser must be prepared to support the decision to exclude data or analysis that might appear to be relevant to the client, intended users, or one's peers. For example, the omission of the cost approach when the appraiser's peer might likely include it, or when intended users might expect to see it, will call for a solid explanation. The appraiser needs to be prepared to provide one. In other words, the burden of proof is on the appraiser in selecting the right scope of work for the assignment at hand.

The Scope of Work Rule goes on, in this section, to say that the scope of work can't be limited so that the assignment results are no longer credible, given the intended use. If, for example, the appraiser cannot obtain relevant information to complete the assignment, the appraiser must (1) withdraw from the assignment, (2) expand the scope of work to include the gathering of such information, or (3) if appropriate, complete the analysis on the basis of an extraordinary assumption relating to the missing information.

Regardless, while there is plenty of flexibility in the scope of work decision, an appraiser can never be biased.

Appraiser's Peers

Appraiser's peers is another recently defined term in USPAP.

> APPRAISER'S PEERS: other appraisers who have expertise and competency in the same or a similar type of assignment.

The ultimate test of credibility is whether the appraiser's opinions and conclusions are found to be credible by his or her peers. Similarly, one of the tests of whether the scope of work decision is appropriate is what one's peers' actions would be in the same or a similar assignment.

There are two important implications regarding an appraiser's peers. First, an appraiser must with his or her peers to find out what they are doing in similar assignments. Second, the appraiser must be able (competent) to recognize what it takes to produce credible assignment results.

Dissecting the Appraisal Process

USPAP says a scope of work decision is acceptable when it is consistent with intended users' expectations and with what our peers' actions would be in the same of similar assignment. But in practice, what are the possibilities when it comes to varying the scope of work?

On the following pages are a series of tables. Each table displays a piece of the appraisal process, or, in the final table, the appraisal review process. That part of the process is then dissected into various steps that comprise it, as shown in the columns. The scope of work possibilities for each step are listed in each column, from the least intensive to the most intensive.

As you can see, there are many ways to slice and dice the appraisal process and the appraisal review process. For each part of the process, there are decisions to be made regarding the scope of work to be applied. You will probably realize that none of this is new—you've been making these decisions all along, in every assignment you've ever taken on.

Table 6.1: Identification of Relevant Real Property Characteristics

Process:	Physical	Legal (e.g., zoning)	Economic (e.g., actual gross income)
Least Intensive	No inspection.*	No research.*	Obtain from owner.*
	Drive-by inspection*	Examine zoning maps*	Read lease(s)
	Drive-by inspection with exterior measurements*	Talk to planning/ zoning department*	Read lease(s), verify with management company
Most Intensive	Interior inspection, with exterior measurements	Talk to planning/ zoning department, obtain and read zoning ordinance	Read lease(s), verify with management company and tenants

* Extraordinary assumptions will need to be stated about information taken to be true when it is uncertain.

Table 6.2: Development of an Opinion About the Quality of Another Appraiser's Work (Appraisal Review)

Process:

Least Intensive	Opinion formed about a portion of an appraisal report only (e.g., discounted cash flow analysis or selection of comparables in sales comparison approach)
	Opinion formed about the quality of an entire appraisal report, with no opinion by the reviewer about value
	Opinion formed about the quality of an entire appraisal report with the reviewer's own opinion of value but based on data presented in report under review (and based on extraordinary assumptions regarding the accuracy of this data)
Most Intensive	Opinion formed about the quality of an entire appraisal report with the reviewer's own opinion of value and verification and analysis of that data

Table 6.3: Application of the Three Approaches to Value

Process:	Cost Approach	Sales Comparison Approach	Income Approach
Least Intensive	Not necessary; omitted	Not necessary; omitted	Not necessary; omitted
	Land valuation via extraction, comparable cost data from readily available sources	Comparable data from files; no adjustments to comparables in analysis	Comparable rental, expense and vacancy data from files; capitalization rates from readily available sources
	Comparable cost data from cost manual but verified	Comparable data from readily available sources, confirmed with one or more parties to the transaction; adjustments supportable	Comparable data, including capitalization rates from readily available sources; confirmed with one or more parties to the transaction
Most Intensive	Land valuation via sales comparison approach with complete verification of sales information; comparable cost data obtained from local contractors	Thorough search of all available data sources; confirmation with one or more parties to the transaction; adjustments via paired sales analysis	Thorough search of all available data sources; confirmation with one or more parties to the transaction local vacancy survey

Table 6.4: Development of Highest and Best Use Opinion (Market Value Appraisals)

Process:

Least Intensive	Inferred, based on readily observed evidence such as surrounding land uses, age and condition of existing improvements, and known market demand for property type*
	Application of four tests (physically possible, legally permissible, financially feasible, maximally productive) but based on readily observed evidence*
	Application of four tests (physically possible, legally permissible, financially feasible, maximally productive) with research into each factor, testing for feasibility
Most Intensive	Application of four tests (physically possible, legally permissible, financially feasible, maximally productive) with complete market analysis and feasibility study

* Extraordinary assumptions may need to be stated about information taken to be true when it is uncertain.

Three Assignments, Same Property

Consider how the following three assignments illustrate the flexibility and opportunities provided under the current USPAP scope of work concept.

Assignment 1

The owner of a single-family residence calls to ask if you can help him out. He is thinking about borrowing against the equity in his home so that he can purchase a boat. He's owned his home for a long time and has no idea what it is currently worth or how much equity he might have in it. He finds your company in the telephone book and calls you because you're a designated member of the Appraisal Institute. He tells you he doesn't need an appraisal; he just wants a rough idea of the value of his house. He doesn't want you to go to a lot of trouble, and he doesn't need a written report. You inform him that an appraisal will need to be ordered by the lender if he applies for a loan. He says he understands that.

Assignment 2

Two weeks later, a lender calls and requests an appraisal of the same property based on an exterior-only inspection (colloquially known as a drive-by) to be completed within three days. For this relatively small, low-risk loan, the lender would like for you to use its short-form report format, developed in-house.

Assignment 3

Seven months later, an attorney calls to order an appraisal for the property settlement in a divorce involving the owners of the same property. The case is going to court, and the appraisal will be used by both sides to settle the question of property value. The attorney requests a thorough inspection of the home and needs an in-depth study of the comparable sales in the market. He says it is important to verify all sales information with county records as well as sellers, buyers, real estate agents, and any other parties to the transaction. The attorney requests that the appraiser do a complete analysis of the market and sales data. The report must contain a detailed description of the subject property, the sales, and the appraisal process used in arriving at an opinion of value.

Table 6.5: Identity of the Intended Use, Intended User, and Type of Value for Each Assignment

	Assignment 1	Assignment 2	Assignment 3
Intended Use	To evaluate equity position	To make a lending decision in a relatively low-risk transaction	To provide the basis for property settlement in a litigated divorce
Intended User(s)	Owner	Lender	Attorney and his client
Type of Value	Market value, possibly expressed as a range	Market value as defined in the appraisal requirements pursuant to FIRREA	Market value as defined by whom?

Table 6.6: Degree of Research and Data Collection Necessary in Each Assignment

	Assignment 1	Assignment 2	Assignment 3
Inspection/ Identification	No inspection ("desktop")	Exterior inspection ("drive-by")	Interior and exterior, thorough
Physical and Economic Factors	Several extraordinary assumptions will be necessary with regard to uncertain but relevant property characteristics such as size, condition, and other property characteristics	Some information concerning relevant property characteristics will be obtained from visual, exterior inspection. Some extraordinary assumptions will be necessary with regard to uncertain but relevant property characteristics.	Most information concerning relevant property characteristics will be obtained from visual, exterior inspection. Virtually no extraordinary assumptions will be used with regard to uncertain but relevant property characteristics.
Extent of Data Research	Data used in prior assignments	Readily available data	Exhaustive search

Table 6.7: Type and Level of Analysis, Given the Intended Use of Each Assignment			
	Assignment 1	**Assignment 2**	**Assignment 3**
Type of Analysis	Sales comparison approach only	Sales comparison approach only	All three approaches
Extent of Analysis	No adjustment process	Adjustments reasonably supportable	In-depth. Adjustments supported using paired sales

Table 6.8: Type of Report Appropriate for Each Assignment			
	Assignment 1	**Assignment 2**	**Assignment 3**
Report	Oral	Brief Summary Appraisal Report using bank's form	Self-Contained Appraisal Report

These assignments involve the same property; however, there are three different intended uses and three different intended users, which create different assignments with three different degrees of research and analysis.

With regard to these three assignments:

- All three assignments meet the needs of their respective intended users.
- All three are credible, given the scope of work.
- All three are accurate.
- All three are reliable for their respective intended uses.
- All three are relevant to the intended use.
- The dates of value can be the same or different.

Especially noteworthy is the fact that the values may be different in each example, even though the same property was appraised.

Chapter 7

Scope Disclosure: What to Report, Why, and How

You've identified the problem to be solved. You've determined the appropriate scope of work. You've developed your analyses, opinions and conclusions. Now it's time to prepare a written report, or present an oral one. What do you say about scope?

Let's first examine the USPAP requirements. The Scope of Work Rule includes the following section:

Essentially, the requirement is to disclose what you did in developing the assignment results. You might also need to disclose what you didn't do.

Reporting Requirements Revisited

It is never enough to communicate only your value opinion. Even for the briefest report, USPAP requires that certain other information accompany the value opinion when it is communicated. It includes:

- Who hired you?

- Who is intended to rely on your expert opinion?
- For what intended use?
- What type of assignment results?
- As of what date?
- What property?
- Given what extraordinary assumptions or hypothetical conditions?

The list above constitutes the seven parameters. Together with the scope of work, they provide the parameters for the assignment and the proper context for the value opinion. Without them, the value opinion alone is meaningless at best, misleading at worst.

Even if only an oral or verbal report is provided to the client, these seven parameters need to be mentioned.

The Appraisal Institute has developed templates for written reports, a Restricted Use Appraisal Report template and a Summary Appraisal Report template (See Appendix A and Appendix B.) They are intended to meet the minimum requirements set forth in USPAP for Restricted Use and Summary Appraisal reports. You can use them as the foundation for creating your own formats, which you can then modify to fit a variety of different situations. Be aware that certain clients or client groups might have additional reporting requirements, and you must modify these formats to allow for them.

The appraiser's responsibility in reporting the appraisal is to the intended user(s).

The report must contain sufficient information so that the intended users can understand it properly and not be misled. This means you are responsible for telling the intended user(s) what you did, why you did what you did, and if anyone helped you in the appraisal process.

- *What you did.*
  In a Self-Contained Appraisal Report, you must describe sufficient information to disclose to the client and any intended users of the appraisal the scope of work used to develop a credible opinion of value. This is to ensure that the client and intended user(s) are not misled as to the extent of work performed by the appraiser.

In a Summary Appraisal Report, you must also summarize what you did, how you did it, and who helped you in the process.

In a Restricted Use Appraisal Report, you must state the extent of the process of collecting, confirming, and reporting data or refer to an assignment agreement in the workfile that describes the scope of work to be performed.

- *Why you did what you did.*
  The burden of proof is on you as the appraiser to support the scope of work decision and the level of information included (or, in some cases, not included) in the report. USPAP doesn't require the appraiser to include this information in the report, but it does require the appraiser to be prepared to support the scope of work decision. Many times, however, it's advisable to include a discussion of why you did what you did in order to be very clear and not misleading.

- *Who helped you in the appraisal process.*
  If someone provided you with significant real property appraisal assistance, you must name him or her in the certification, and in your scope of work discussion you must describe what he or she did.

Standards Rules 2-2(a)(vii), 2-2(b)(vii), 2-2(c)(vii) address these requirements.

The content of a Self-Contained Appraisal Report must be consistent with the intended use of the appraisal and, at a minimum:

describe the scope of work used to develop the appraisal;

<u>Comment</u>: Because intended users' reliance on an appraisal may be affected by the scope of work, the report must enable them to be properly informed and not misled. Sufficient information includes disclosure of research and analyses performed and might also include disclosure of research and analyses not performed.

When any portion of the work involves significant real property appraisal assistance, the appraiser must describe the extent of that assistance. The signing appraiser must also state the name(s) of those providing the significant real property appraisal assistance in the certification, in accordance with SR 2-3.

The content of a Summary Appraisal Report must be consistent with the intended use of the appraisal and, at a minimum:

summarize the scope of work used to develop the appraisal;

<u>Comment</u>: Because intended users' reliance on an appraisal may be affected by the scope of work, the report must enable them to be properly informed and not misled. Sufficient information includes disclosure of research and analy-

ses performed and might also include disclosure of research and analyses not performed.

When any portion of the work involves significant real property appraisal assistance, the appraiser must summarize the extent of that assistance. The signing appraiser must also state the name(s) of those providing the significant real property appraisal assistance in the certification, in accordance with SR 2-3.

The content of a Restricted Use Appraisal Report must be consistent with the intended use of the appraisal and, at a minimum:

state the scope of work used to develop the appraisal;

Comment: Because intended users' reliance on an appraisal may be affected by the scope of work, the report must enable them to be properly informed and not misled. Sufficient information includes disclosure of research and analyses performed, and might also include disclosure of research and analyses not performed.

When any portion of the work involves significant real property appraisal assistance, the appraiser must summarize the extent of that assistance. The signing appraiser must also state the name(s) of those providing the significant real property appraisal assistance in the certification, in accordance with SR 2-3.

Where Does the Discussion Belong in a Written Report?

USPAP does not specify a location for the scope of work disclosure. Generally, it's best to have a separate section of the report entitled Scope of Work. This practice makes it easy for the reader to locate the disclosure.

Alternatively, the scope of work discussion can be placed throughout the report, within the sections that address those portions of the appraisal process. The detail on the scope is therefore specific to each section.

A third way is a combination of the two: A general disclosure can be located in a separate section, and more detailed discussions can be located in the appropriate sections of the report.

Beyond the requirement to be clear and not misleading, where you place the discussion of scope of work in the appraisal report is a matter of style. Take note of how other professional reports are written (for example, engineers' reports, building inspection reports, and environmental reports), and follow the lead of those that impress you most.

Don't forget: The scope of work is a critical step in the appraisal process. The manner in which you address scope in your report should underscore its importance. In the briefest of appraisal reports, the scope of work discussion might well comprise the bulk of the report.

General Assumptions or Scope?

Consider whether some of the items typically included as Assumptions and Limiting Conditions are actually scope of work matters.

Let's review some of the statements that are commonly included as Assumptions and Limiting Conditions statements. Should some of these issues be addressed under scope of work instead?

> **Assumptions and Limiting Conditions**
> This appraisal report has been made with the following assumptions and limiting conditions:
>
> > This is a Summary Appraisal Report, which is intended to comply with the reporting requirements set forth under Standards Rule 2-2(b) of the Uniform Standards of Professional Appraisal Practice for a Summary Appraisal Report. As such, it presents only summary discussions of the data, reasoning, and analyses that were used in the appraisal process to develop the appraiser's opinion of value. Supporting documentation that is not provided with the report concerning the data, reasoning, and analyses is retained in the appraiser's file. The depth of discussion contained in this report is specific to the needs of the client and for the intended use stated in the report. The appraiser is not responsible for unauthorized use of this report.

This is a statement of the report options used. Including such a statement is a USPAP requirement. While it's not a scope issue, it might be better placed in a letter of transmittal, if there is one.

> The legal description furnished is assumed to be correct. The appraiser assumes no responsibility for matters legal in character, nor renders any opinion as to the title, which is assumed to be good.

This is a general assumption, but it could be included as part of the scope statement.

> The property was appraised as having knowledgeable ownership and competent management.

This is a general assumption, but it could be included as part of the scope statement.

> The appraiser has made no survey and assumes no responsibility in connection with such matters.

This is a general assumption, but it could be included as part of the scope statement.

This is a general assumption, but it could be included as part of the scope statement.

This is a general assumption, but it could be included as part of the scope statement.

This is a general assumption, but it could be included as part of the scope statement.

This is a general assumption, but it could be included as part of the scope statement.

This is a general assumption, but it could be included as part of the scope statement.

This is an attempt to limit the client's use of the report. Such language is unnecessary, however, because stating the intended users and intended use suffices, for the most part. Generally, clients can do what they want with the reports once they have received them. If the appraiser wants to prevent the client from disseminating the report in some manner, the appraiser must get the client's agreement on that matter at the time of the assignment.

Sample Statements to Be Included in the Scope of Work Disclosure

The following are illustrations of possible statements to be included in the scope of work disclosure of a report. These statements have been divided into the four major sections:

- Extent to which the property is identified
- Extent to which the property is inspected
- Type and extent of the data researched
- Type and extent of analysis applied

> Be careful to avoid using "boilerplate" in your scope discussions. The whole idea is to tailor the scope to the particular assignment.

These are not in themselves complete scope discussions; they are merely excerpts from complete scope discussions.

These individual statements are not the only ways to state the scope issues; they are just several of many ways. You may well be able to improve upon them in terms of wording or style. Appraisers should develop individual statements for each assignment or type of assignment.

Extent to Which the Property Is Identified

Physical characteristics

- In this appraisal assignment, I viewed the interior and exterior of the subject improvements in order to gather information about the physical characteristics of the subject improvements that are relevant to the valuation problem.

- Information about the scope and character of the proposed improvements is based on plans prepared by (name) and dated mm/dd/yy.

Legal characteristics

- I relied on the title report prepared by (name) on mm/dd/yy for information regarding easements, covenants, restrictions, and other encumbrances. I did not research the presence of such items independently.

Economic characteristics

- I examined the lease between (lessor) and (lessee) dated dd/mm/yy concerning the subject property to identify its terms and conditions.

Extent to Which the Property Is Inspected

- I viewed the interior and exterior of the subject property on mm/dd/yy.

- I did not inspect the subject property. Information about the size, condition, and other aspects of the real estate was obtained from a prior appraisal of this property completed by John Doe on mm/dd/yy/. My appraisal is based on the extraordinary assumption that the information in Mr. Doe's appraisal is accurate.

- I viewed only the exterior of the subject property from the street on mm/dd/yy.

- This appraisal is based on the extraordinary assumption that the interior of the subject property is (typical of the area, similar to the previous appraisal, average for the market, in good condition, as indicated on the assessor's records). If this assumption is not true, the value of the property may be affected.

- I used information from county records, a previous appraisal of the subject property, real estate agent, owner's comments, buyer's description, assessor's records, the state records, multiple listing service data, brochures, and leasing data sheets to identify the characteristics of the subject property that are relevant to the valuation problem."

Type and Extent of the Data Researched

- Sales of similar properties that have occurred over the past (time period) were researched in (geographic area).

- I researched data on comparable land and improved sales, income and expense information, and construction costs; confirmed all comparable sales information; and analyzed the information gathered in applying the cost, sales comparison, and income capitalization approaches.

- The cost approach requires the assemblage of recent land sales for comparison. In order to gather the comparable sales, I consulted county records, assessors, brokers, investors, and lenders active in the area.

- I located xx sales, xx pending sales, and xx listings in the market area searched. Comparables were selected based on physical and location characteristics. Of these sales, the xx considered to be most similar were used in the sales comparison approach because.

- I verified the data with (name the parties).

- I searched the subject market area for (land or improved) sales of properties with industrial, commercial, or residential, (or be more specific) zoning. There were several sales within the immediate area of the subject property. I selected xx of those sales considered to be the most similar to the subject property because…

- In the cost approach either replacement or reproduction cost is used to develop a value indication for the subject property. Due to the age and construction style of the improvements, the replacement cost was used in this analysis. The replacement cost for the subject property has been estimated via the cost-estimating service technique using (name of service), adjusted for local costs.

- In order to arrive at an opinion of the market value of the subject property, I researched the market for (manufacturing, warehouse, and duplex) buildings. Because I found no sales in the subject's market area, it was necessary to expand the search to the (village, town, city, county, or state). The sales selected were considered competitive with the subject property. These sales reflect what buyers are willing to pay for (a certain type of) properties.

Type and Extent of Analysis Applied

- The value opinions presented in this report are based upon review and analysis of the market conditions affecting real property value, including land values, cost and depreciation estimates, the attributes of competitive properties, and sales data for (residential, commercial, and industrial) properties.

- In order to determine the highest and best use of the real estate, I completed a survey of the market, carefully noting supply and demand factors, and examined the feasibility of alternative uses.

- The appraisal problem did not warrant an intensive highest and best use study. Given the nature of the subject real estate, my conclusion of highest and best use was based on logic and observed evidence.

- I have considered all three approaches and then reconciled them to arrive at a final opinion of value for the subject property.

- There are three traditional approaches used to arrive at an opinion of value of real estate: the sales comparison approach, the cost approach, and the income capitalization approach. All three approaches to value were used to arrive at an opinion of the market value of the subject property as of the date of this appraisal.

- After selecting the sales, a comparative analysis of relevant factors that influence value was undertaken to adjust the sales to the subject property based upon the actions and preferences demonstrated by the participants in the marketplace.

- Three approaches to value have been used in arriving at an opinion of value of the leased fee (fee simple) interest in the subject property. In the reconciliation, I considered the quantity and quality of the data available under each approach, the advantages and/or the disadvantages of each approach, and the relevance of each to the subject property and the appraisal problem.

- I did not apply the (cost/sales comparison/income) approach because it was not considered applicable to arrive at credible results. I applied the (cost/sales comparison/income) approaches, which are necessary for credible results given the intended use, property characteristics, and type of value sought.

Sample Scope of Work Discussions

The pages that follow show excerpts of scope of work discussions from written appraisal reports. These are not perfect examples, but they are acceptable for scope of work discussions. They are intended to give some idea as to what to say and how to say it and should be viewed as a starting point only. You will probably find ways to improve upon them.

Scope of Work in a Condemnation Assignment

The scope of work in this assignment included a personal inspection of the subject property, reviewing public record information concerning the subject and other properties in its immediate neighborhood, reviewing FDOT R/W maps and construction plans associated with this road widening project, and searching for sales of vacant and improved properties similar to the subject in both the "before" and "after" situations. Due to the large number of sales (both vacant and improved) in the PlaceName Shores subdivision, this search for comparable sales was concentrated in, but not limited to, this subdivision. The search extended retroactively two years for interior sales and five years for sales with frontage along XXX River Boulevard. All sales used in comparison to the subject were personally inspected (exterior only, unless otherwise noted) by the appraiser and were photographed by either the appraiser or someone under his direction. To assist in determining what effect, if any, the proposed acquisition may have on the remainder, the scope of this assignment also included searching other neighborhoods for sales of properties that may have been affected by similar acquisitions.

The scope of work for this assignment also included developing opinions of value of the subject in both the before and after situations using the cost approach. Cost new is based on information obtained from

Marshall & Swift *Residential Cost Handbook* as well as information obtained from local builders. Depreciation is estimated based on abstractions from sales of similar sales in the PlaceName Shores Subdivision.

Sources used in obtaining sale information included: public records (deed recording, City of XYZ data, tax assessment records), real estate sales data published by First American Real Estate Services, IRIS, MLS data, other appraisers, local real estate sales agents, and field inspections and verifications of comparable properties. Market data gathered include sales and listings of properties with single-family residential use potential. All of the sales data used in this appraisal were verified by contacting and interviewing the property owners, principals to transactions, or public officials. All sales applied in the analyses are described in detail on Sale Summary sheets included in the addendum to this report. Sketches and maps of each sale are also included as part of each sale write-up.

The scope of this assignment does not include apportioning the value of the acquisition between any parties that may have an interest.

Scope of Work for an Appraisal Quality Assessment

(Review of an Appraisal Completed for HUD)

- Receipt and review of the entire appraisal report provided to HUD by the lender noted on page one of Form 1004, which was used to insure financing for the borrower

- Personal on-site, interior inspection of the subject property

- Personal inspection and photographing of all comparables cited in the report under review

- Verification of subject and comparable data

- Personal inspection and photographing of comparable sales deemed more appropriate than those used within the subject appraisal

- Development of any applicable approaches to value that were not adequately developed in the subject appraisal report, and reporting of the reviewer's analysis and conclusions in the review report

- Documenting all deficiencies found in the appraisal report

- Completion of the appropriate Appraisal Quality Assessment Report Form 1038

Scope of Work for a Lending Assignment

(As Described in a Proposal Letter)

The appraiser

a. will inspect the subject property to note the characteristics of the property that are relevant to its valuation;

b. will investigate available market data for use in a sales comparison approach to value and, if appropriate, cost and income capitalization approaches.

    The appraiser's investigations will include research of public records through the use of commercial sources of data such as printed comparable data services and computerized databases. Search parameters such as dates of sales, leases, locations, sizes, types of properties, and distances from the subject will start with relatively narrow constraints and, if necessary, be expanded until the appraiser has either retrieved data sufficient (in the appraiser's opinion) to estimate market value, or until the appraiser believes that he or she has reasonably exhausted the available pool of data. Researched sales data will be viewed and, if found to be appropriate, efforts will be made to verify the data with persons directly involved in the transactions such as buyers, seller, brokers, or agents. At the appraiser's discretion, some data will be used without personal verification if, in the appraiser's opinion, the data appear to be correct. In addition, the appraiser will consider any appropriate listings or properties found through observation during appraiser's data collection process. The appraiser will report only the data deemed to be pertinent to the valuation problem;

c. will investigate and analyze any pertinent easements or restrictions, on the fee simple ownership of the subject property. It is the client's responsibility to supply the appraiser with a title report. If a title report is not available, the appraiser will rely on a visual inspection and identify any readily apparent easements or restrictions;

d. will analyze the data found and reach conclusions regarding the market value, as defined in the report, of the subject property as of the date of value using appropriate valuation approach (es) identified above;

e. will prepare the appraisal in compliance with the Uniform Standards of Professional Appraisal Practice as promulgated by The Appraisal Foundation and the Code of Professional Ethics and Certification Standard of the Appraisal Institute;

f. will not be responsible for ascertaining the existence of any toxic waste or other contamination present on or off the site. The appraiser will, however, report any indications of toxic waste or contaminants that may affect value if they are readily apparent during appraiser's investigations. Appraiser cautions the user of the report that appraiser is not expert in such matters and that appraiser may overlook contamination that might be readily apparent to parties who are experts in such matters.

g. will prepare a Summary Appraisal Report, as defined in USPAP, which will include photographs of the subject property, descriptions of the subject neighborhood, the site, any improvements on the site, a description of the zoning, a highest and best use analysis, a summary of the most important sales used in the appraiser's valuation, a reconciliation and conclusion, a map illustrating the sales in relationship to the subject property, and other data deemed by the appraiser to be relevant to the assignment. Pertinent data and analyses not included in the report may be retained in appraiser's files.

Scope of Work for an Assignment Involving a Proposed Easement

The problem to be solved is to identify the market influence of a particular flood easement located on the subject property. Specifically, the problem includes ascertaining the diminution in value (if any) directly related to the easement. The surest method of analysis is a comparison of the property under two scenarios. The first scenario assumes a hypothetical condition with no flood easement, and the second scenario values the property in its present "as is" condition *with* the flood easement. This is a logical approach to the problem and most closely represents actual market events.

After consulting with the client, it was determined that the assignment would be divided into two phases. The first provides for opinions of value according to the two scenarios, developed using a narrow scope of work. If the client's matter is settled, the second phase will be unnecessary. However, if the client's matter is not settled, the appraiser will take on the second phase. In the second phase, opinions of value, according to the two scenarios, will be developed under a broad scope of work, ready for trial purposes.

In both phases the property is valued, both with and without the flood easement. The difference between the two values is attributable to the influence of the flood easement. Any resulting diminution in value will typically include the loss of property rights within the easement area and any buyer reluctance attributable to the easement. The latter analysis will include an extraordinary assumption (i.e., it assumes any existing improvements are located outside the flood easement). Otherwise, a cloud on title might be created, and analysis of that condition would be outside the scope of this assignment.

The scope of work for the first phase does not involve all of the analytical tools available to an appraiser but still affords the client meaningful information for making an initial decision. The market value *with* the flood easement will be provided as a range in value. The analyses will be refined further, if necessary, in the second phase.

The second phase includes preparation of an appraisal that is trial-ready. This analysis, presented in a Self-Contained Appraisal Report, will include survey interviews of potential and actual buyers to gauge their reaction to the issues of the flood easement. This additional information will be reconciled with the market data. All applicable approaches and analyses will be included in this second phase.

Scope of Work for an Assignment Involving an Assessment for Replacement of Public Utilities

The subject property is improved with public utilities, including public water and sewer. City engineers have recently determined that these utilities must be replaced due to normal wear and tear. As part of the reconstruction project, the existing roadbed will be replaced once the new utilities in the street have been installed. The project will take about one year to complete.

The problem to be solved is identifying the change in the subject's market value that is attributable directly to the reconstruction project. The city can assess the apportioned cost of the project to the subject property, but that amount cannot exceed the increased benefit in market value according to the current law. The client's concern is that the city's assessment does not exceed the benefit in market value attributed to the reconstruction project.

The value before reconstruction is an "as is" market value since the project is proposed and no work has commenced. The market value after the reconstruction of the street, however, is based on a hypothetical condition.

The estimate of the "before" value is a straightforward analysis using historical sales in the immediate area similar to the subject property. In contrast, the after value identifies nearby comparable market areas that have newly reconstructed streets. After pairing up similar properties and adjusting for differences in features, the remaining disparity in value can be attributed to the improved street and utilities. This difference, however, is then crosschecked with interviews of each buyer in the newly improved area. Specifically, the interviews will ascertain what role the reconstructed street played in the buyer's purchase decision. This information will be reconciled with the sales comparison study that compared areas with existing improvements to other areas with reconstructed streets.

Scope of Work for a Valuation for Financial Reporting Assignment (as Described in an Engagement Letter)

Mr. Controller
Company A
Address
City, State Zip Code
Date

Dear Mr. Controller:

We appreciate the opportunity to confirm your authorization for 123 Appraisal Company to provide our consulting services in conjunction with the review of Company A's modeling and calculation of impairment related to their office building known as ABC Office Building, located at XYZ Asset Street, Market City, ST. We understand that our analysis and comments will be used to assist management and their audit advisors in reaching a determination of the impairment created by Company A's current lease commitments at ABC Office Building.

We have not been engaged to make specific purchase or sale recommendations. Our work is designed to provide information that will allow you to make a more informed decision in developing future strategies.

Scope of the Engagement

The objective of our assignment is to assist Company A with regard to the following:

1. What is the market rent for ABC Office Building, including lease term and tenant improvement budgets?
2. What will be the lease-up/absorption period?
3. What will be the applicable market rent growth to be expected for ABC Office Building over the holding period of the lease term?
4. What are reasonable operating expenses for the project, once released?

It is our understanding that management will use the results of this information to incorporate into a model that in turn will calculate the current impairment to Company A's leasehold position in ABC Office Building.

123 Appraisal Company is not completing a valuation of Company A's leasehold position. Nor will 123 Appraisal Company have any direct input into the cash flow model being created by Company A and its reliability.

Our work will be performed in compliance with the Uniform Standards of Professional Appraisal Practice (USPAP) and with the Code of Professional Ethics of the Appraisal Institute.

Availability of Data

We will need access to all requested information to ensure successful and timely completion of the engagement.

The following information will be required and must be available on a timely basis to complete the engagement as scheduled:

- Property marketing plan
- Access to the broker marketing the property
- Current lease(s) in place
- Summary of current tenant improvement dollars spent
- Remaining tenant improvement budget, and
- Access to the buildings

Personnel

123 Appraiser will serve as the Engagement Partner for this engagement. He will provide the analysis and conclusions on behalf of 123 Appraisal Company. Credentials are attached. One staff consultant will provide assistance in conducting market interviews and research.

Timing

It is our understanding that time is of the essence. As discussed, we are prepared to begin work immediately. We estimate that within a week to 10 days, we will be able to provide our analysis and comments.

This estimate assumes that we receive full access to the required information detailed above.

Reporting

We will present our findings in a brief report for the initial phase of this assignment, describing the purpose and scope of our analysis, a brief description of the project included, and the premise of work. We will discuss the information used and methodologies applied to derive at our results. This document will be subject to our statement of limiting terms and conditions, which is attached.

Fees and Billing Arrangements

We have analyzed the professional resources required to complete the proposed engagement within the timeframe stipulated and, based on the level of limited reporting requested, we estimate a fee in the range of $fee to $fee.

Out-of-pocket expenses—including costs incurred for travel/subsistence, word processing, report production, telephone calls, facsimile transmission, and delivery charges—will be extra. Additional consultation after the completion of our valuation related to meetings and expert testimony, if necessary, will incur additional fees to be separately arranged.

Upon the completion of the assignment, we will submit an invoice for all fees and any out-of-pocket expenses incurred. We shall keep you informed of any circumstances that affect the scope of our services, the timetable for delivery, or the level of fees incurred. Our bills are payable upon receipt and due within 30 days. Interest computed at a rate of x.x% per month will be charged on all bills not paid within 30 days.

    We appreciate this opportunity to be of service and look forward to working with you on this engagement. We can assure you that we are committed to completing this project in an efficient and timely manner. Should you have any questions regarding this proposal, please call 123 Appraiser at 000-123-4567.

Very truly yours,
123 Appraiser
123 Appraisal Company

On the pages that follow are examples of assignments and discussions of how they might be handled. In an increasingly complex business environment, appraisers are faced with new opportunities involving a broad variety of issues because their clients are confronted with a broad variety of problems.

As you read through these case studies, keep in mind the three steps to the problem-solving process: identify the problem, plan the solution, and apply the solution. Observe how critical it is to complete each of those steps—and in the correct order.

Some of these case studies pertain to residential properties while others pertain to commercial and industrial properties. Read through each case study no matter what type of property you typically appraise. The principles are the same, regardless of the property type.

These are only a few of the possible assignments an appraiser might be requested to complete. Studying these, however, will give you insights into the correct handling of other situations that might arise.

Case Study 1: "Exterior Only" Inspection, Residential Property

The Request

Lender A asks your availability, fee, and turnaround time for a drive-by appraisal.

The Consultation

You clarify that the only inspection is to be from the curb. Lender A tells you that the owner says it's a 2,500-sq.-ft. home on a half-acre lot with 4 bedrooms and 2 baths and was built in 1986. Lender A believes a sales comparison approach alone is adequate, and requests that you use the standard Form 2055. So this is a relatively low-risk transaction you ask. Lender A says it's a home equity loan, and the borrower has owned the home for a long time and probably has lots of equity in it.

Identification of the Problem

Client: Lender A

Intended User: Lender A

Intended Use: To assist the client in making a lending decision

Type of Opinion: Market value, according to the definition that is printed on Form 2055

Effective Date: Current date

Relevant Characteristics About the Subject: The single-family residence is located at 123 Main St., is approx. 2,500 square feet, has 4 bedrooms, 2 baths, sits on a half-acre lot, and was built in 1986. Fee simple interest.

Assignment Conditions: Supplemental standards: FNMA guidelines for Form 2055 drive-by appraisal. Extraordinary assumption: That the improvements comprise 2,500 square feet, 4 bedrooms, and 2 baths, and the overall property condition is typical of the market area.

Scope of Work Plan

Check on-line county records to see if they indicate that the subject is approximately 2,500 square feet, and the lot is a half-acre. When the subject house is viewed from the curb, check to see if it appears to be 2,500 square feet. As long as there is no reason to believe otherwise, the appraisal will assume that it is 2,500 square feet. Also, when you view the property from the curb, note observable features and overall condition.

Search for comparable sales in the MLS, on-line county records, and office files. Drive by the comparables. If the reported sales prices in the MLS are inconsistent with the county records, contact the sales agent to clarify.

Search the county records for information about any sales of subject within the last three years. If there are such sales, analyze them relative to the current appraised value.

Scope of Work Discussion in Report

I viewed the subject property from the curb only. The scope of this assignment did not include a walk through of the interior. Information about the size, room count, and overall condition of the improvements was provided by the client and checked against county records. This appraisal is based on the extraordinary assumption that the improvements comprise 2500 square feet, has 4 bedrooms and 2 baths, and that the overall property condition is typical of the market area. If this assumption were false, then the value indications in this appraisal would be different.

I used the Multiple Listing Service (MLS) to compile sales data. I also searched county records and my own data files. When information from these sources was inconsistent or lacking, I conferred with the selling agent involved in the transaction to clarify.

The cost and income approaches to value were not considered necessary in this assignment and were not performed.

Case Study 2: "Exterior Only" Inspection, Commercial Property

The Request

Lender B requests a "limited-summary" appraisal of an owner-user office building.

The Consultation

While USPAP no longer includes the term "limited appraisal" (or "complete appraisal"), you and your client can still converse in those terms if they are useful to you. But what does the client mean by "limited"? In this case, the client states that access to the interior of the property is not available because this is a pre-foreclosure situation and the borrower/occupant is not cooperative. So the only inspection will be from the curb. Lender B does not expect the cost or income approaches to be necessary in this assignment and will provide you with their most recent appraisal of the property that was prepared by another appraiser three years ago. This appraisal indicates that the improvements consist of a 3,264-sq.-ft., Class D, single-user office building constructed in 1964 and renovated in 1998. The report states that the site is 6,500 square feet, approximately, and is zoned C-2. The property is located on the fringe of the urban core but near a major highway interchange.

Identification of the Problem

Client: Lender B

Intended User: Lender B

Intended Use: To assist the client in evaluating collateral in a pre-foreclosure situation

Type of Opinion: Market value, according to definition in the appraisal requirements pursuant to FIRREA

Effective Date: Current date

Relevant Characteristics About the Subject: The office property is located at 456 Broad St., is a 3,264-sq.-ft., single-user building constructed in 1964, and was renovated in 1998. It sits on a 6,500-sq.-ft. lot zoned C-2. Fee simple interest.

Assignment Conditions: Supplemental standards: Appraisal requirements pursuant to FIRREA. Extraordinary assumption: That the improvements are as described in the prior appraisal report prepared by (name) and dated mm/dd/yy, and that the property condition is typical for the market area.

Scope of Work Plan

When you drive by the subject, check to see that it appears to be as described in the prior appraisal report and that the property condition appears to be typical of the market area. As long as there is no reason to believe otherwise, the appraisal will assume so. Also, when you drive by the property, note observable features and its overall condition.

Search for comparable sales in county records and office files. Also contact commercial sales agents who you know deal with this property type in the area. Contact appraisers who you know appraise these property types. View potential comparables from the curb.

Search county records for information about any sales of subject within the last three years. If there are such sales, analyze them relative to the current appraised value.

Scope of Work Discussion in Report

I viewed the property from the curb only. The scope of this assignment did not include a walk-through of the interior. Information about property features such as size and layout was obtained from the appraisal report dated mm/dd/yy by (name) as provided by the client. My appraisal is based on the extraordinary assumptions that (1) the information in the prior appraisal by (name) about the subject property is accurate, and that (2) the property condition is typical of its market area. If this assumption were false, then the value indications in this appraisal would be different.

I searched county records and my own date files for comparable information. I also conferred with real estate brokers and other appraisers who work with this property type in this area.

The cost and income approaches to value were not considered necessary in this assignment and were not performed.

Case Study 3: "Desktop" Appraisal, Residential Property

The Request

Lender C requests a "desktop" appraisal for a second mortgage on a single-family residence for which the bank currently holds the first mortgage. She has the appraisal prepared for the first loan and will fax it to you so you can use the information in it about the subject property.

The Consultation

You clarify that there will be no property inspection; you will prepare this assignment "from your desk," based on information about the subject property in the prior appraisal report. Further, you will apply the sales comparison approach only. You clarify with the client that this narrow scope of work will result in a value opinion that is adequately reliable for their intended use, and that a "desktop appraisal form" will be used to report your findings.

Identification of the Problem

Client: Lender C

Intended User: Lender C

Intended Use: To assist the client in making a lending decision

Type of Opinion: Market value, according to definition that is printed on the "desktop" appraisal form

Effective Date: Current date

Relevant Characteristics About the Subject: The single-family residence is located at 789 1st Ave., which, according to the prior appraisal, is approximately 2,000 square feet, 3 bedrooms, 2 baths, located on a 0.25-acre lot, and built in 1990. Fee simple interest.

Assignment Conditions: Supplemental standards: FNMA guidelines for desktop appraisal. Extraordinary assumption: That the improvements comprise 2,000 square feet, 3 bedrooms, and 2 baths, and the overall property condition is typical of the market area.

Scope of Work Plan

Check on-line county records. Do they indicate that the subject is 2,000 square feet, approximately? Is the lot 0.25-acre? As long as there is no reason to believe otherwise, the appraisal will assume it is so.

Search for comparable sales in the MLS, on-line county records, office files. If reported sale prices in MLS are inconsistent with county records, contact sales agent to clarify.

Search county records for information about any sales of the subject within the last three years. If there are such sales, analyze them relative to current appraised value.

Scope of Work Discussion in Report

Case Study 4: "Desktop" Appraisal, Commercial Property

The Request

Party X recently inherited a retail property in Growingtown. He found you through the Appraisal Institute's Web site. He tells you, "I don't need an appraisal. I just want to know what I've got here. You know, a rough idea of what it's worth. I'm not sure if I want to sell it or hang on to it."

The Consultation

Party X is saying that he doesn't want an appraisal because he holds a very common misconception about what constitutes an appraisal. If you give him your opinion of value—which is what he wants—that *is* an appraisal. But that doesn't necessarily mean an in-depth scope of work to develop the opinion or a lengthy, written appraisal report.

You find out more: The real estate is a 5,000-sq.-ft., free-standing building on a pad site that is part of a neighborhood retail center constructed about five years ago. Growingtown is a small community located about an hour's drive away where several large residential subdivisions have been recently developed. Its population has doubled in the last eight years. The subject property is leased to a nationally known drug store chain on an absolute net basis for a term of 20 years, with rent adjusted every three years according to the CPI. At the end of the 20-year term there are three, five-year renewal options. Party X tells you he'll fax a copy of the lease.

Identification of the Problem

Client: Party X

Intended User: Party X

Intended Use: To assist the owner in deciding whether to hold or dispose of the asset

Type of Opinion: Market value, according to definition in *The Dictionary of Real Estate Appraisal*

Effective Date: Current date

Relevant Characteristics About the Subject: Leased fee interest, according to the lease dated mm/dd/yy between (lessor) and (lessee) in real property located at 123 Main St., Growingtown

Assignment Conditions: Extraordinary assumption: That the improvements are as described: a 5,000-sq.-ft. retail building in good condition on a pad site in XYZ Center in Growingtown

Scope of Work Plan

There is no need to visit the subject property, given the client's intended use and the nature of the property being appraised (a leased fee interest with a long-term lease.) Viewing the property would likely make little or no difference to your opinion of value in this case.

Analyze the lease, noting especially adjustment clauses, expense clauses, and renewal options.

Search for comparable rentals, starting with your own office files. If necessary, contact commercial leasing agents who work the Growingtown area. Compare market rent to contract rent.

Search county records for information about any sales of the subject within last three years. If there are such sales, analyze them relative to current appraised value.

Scope of Work Discussion in Report

The subject property consists of a leased fee interest according to the lease between (lessor) and (lessee). The scope of this assignment did not include a visit to the subject site. My appraisal is based on the extraordinary assumption that the improvements consist of a 5,000-sq.-ft. retail building in good condition on a pad site in XYZ Center in Growingtown.

I researched market rents and capitalization rates using data from my own files and information obtained from leasing agents who work in the Growingtown market area.

The income approach to value was considered the only approach necessary in this assignment.

Case Study 5: "Value in Relation to a Benchmark" Appraisal

The Request

Party N owns and occupies a light industrial facility on the outskirts of town. Party N believes his property is over-assessed at $2.6 million and is looking for your assistance in obtaining a reduction in property taxes. Party N doesn't want to spend a lot of money on an appraisal unless he can get the tax reduction.

The Consultation

You cannot promise Party N that a tax reduction will be the end result. The best approach is to first answer the question, is the market value of the subject property less than $2.6 million? Answering this question is, in itself, the development of an appraisal. But it could require must less work than developing an opinion of value as a pinpoint number.

You can agree with Party N that you'll accept a flat (or hourly) fee for this first phase. You could report the opinion verbally, or if the client wants it in writing, in a Restricted Use Appraisal Report format. Then, should the result of this initial investigation be that, yes, the market value is less than $2.6 million, you would move to a second phase, which is to develop an opinion of market value as a pinpoint number. This second appraisal could be used as the basis to argue the appeal.

Party N tells you that the building is 40,000 square feet with 1,200 square feet of finished office and sits on three acres.

Identification of the Problem

Client: Party N

Intended User: Party N

Intended Use: To assist the client in deciding whether to go forward with a property tax appeal.

Type of Opinion: Market value, according to definition in *The Dictionary of Real Estate Appraisal.*

Effective Date: Current date

Relevant Characteristics About the Subject: A light industrial facility located at 100 Industrial Ave.; 40,000 square feet including 1,200 square feet of finished office space on three acres. Fee simple interest.

Assignment Conditions: Extraordinary assumption: That the improvements comprise 40,000 square feet of light industrial space including

1,200 square feet of finished office, and the overall property condition is typical of the market area.

Scope of Work Plan

Check on-line county records. Do they indicate that the subject is 40,000 square feet, approximately? Observe subject property from curb. Does it appear to be 40,000 square feet? As long as there is no reason to believe otherwise, the appraisal will assume that it is 40,000 square feet. Also, when driving by the property, note observable features and overall condition.

Search for comparable sales and rentals data files, and county records. Contact local sales and leasing agents who work with this property type in the area if needed.

Search county records for information about any sales of the subject within the last three years. If there are such sales, analyze them relative to their current appraised value.

Scope of Work Discussion in Report

The objective of this assignment is to develop an opinion as to whether the market value is less than $2.6 million, which is the current assessed value.

I viewed the property from the curb only. The scope of this assignment did not include a walk-through of the interior. Information about the size and overall condition of the improvements was provided by the client. This appraisal is based on the extraordinary assumption that the improvements comprise 40,000 square feet, including 1,200 square feet of finished office area, and that the overall property condition is typical of the market area. If these assumptions were false, then the value indications in this appraisal would be different.

I searched county records and my own data files. Using these current data, I developed the sales comparison approach, but only to the point that I could draw a conclusion about the current value of the subject in relation to the prior appraised value.

The sales comparison approach is the best approach to value in this assignment, as sales data are relatively plentiful, and properties like the subject are typically purchased by owner occupants, not by investors. The cost and income approaches to value were not considered necessary and were not performed.

Case Study 6: "Recertification of Value" Request

The Request

Lender Z ask you to provide a "recertification" of an appraisal you prepared five months ago.

The Consultation

A true "recertification" is not an appraisal, but a confirmation that the assumptions made in a previously prepared appraisal did, in fact, turn out to be true. For example, an appraisal of proposed improvements might have been made on the basis of an extraordinary assumption that those improvements would be completed as proposed. A recertification would be a confirmation that the improvements were indeed completed as proposed.

Many times the term "recertification" is used inappropriately, however. Often, when clients ask for a "recertification," they really need an opinion that the value is currently at least what it was in the prior appraisal report. This, of course, is a new appraisal (or an "update"). However, in this new appraisal, the value conclusion could be in relation to a benchmark–i.e., a conclusion that yes/no the value is/is not currently at least $X, where $X is the prior appraised value.

Identification of the Problem

Client: Lender X

Intended User: Lender X

Intended Use: To assist the client in making a lending decision

Type of Opinion: Market value according to the appraisal regulations pursuant to FIRREA (or FNMA guidelines). The objective of the appraisal is to develop an opinion as to whether the market value is at least $X, which was the appraiser's opinion of value in a prior appraisal assignment dated mm/dd/yy.

Effective Date: Current date

Relevant Characteristics About the Subject: Property type and characteristics as described in the prior appraisal dated mm/dd/yy. Fee simple interest.

Assignment Conditions: Extraordinary assumption: That the improvements remain as described in the prior appraisal by this appraiser dated mm/dd/yy.

Scope of Work Plan

Refresh your memory about subject property by looking over prior appraisal.

Search for comparable sales in the MLS, on-line county records, and office files. Update the highest and best use analysis and approach (es) to value as necessary using current data. Do so only up to the point that you can conclude whether the current value is at least $X or not.

Search county records for information about any sales of subject since the prior appraisal.

Scope of Work Discussion in Report

The objective of this assignment is to develop an opinion as to whether the market value is at least $X, which was the appraiser's opinion of value in a prior appraisal assignment dated mm/dd/yy. I did not visit the subject site in conjunction with this current analysis. This appraisal is based on the extraordinary assumption that the subject improvements remain as described in the prior appraisal report. If this assumption were false, then the value indications in this appraisal would be different.

I used the Multiple Listing Service (MLS) for compilation of sales data. I also searched county records and my own data files. Using these current data, I re-analyzed my prior highest and best use opinion. I also developed the sales comparison approach but only to the point that I could draw a conclusion about the current value of the subject in relation to the prior appraised value.

The cost and income approaches to value were not considered necessary in this assignment and were not performed.

Case Study 7: Reporting Value Before Completion of Written Report

The Request

You are in the middle of an appraisal assignment involving a very large, complex property. The due date for your report—which will consist of several hundred pages, plus attachments—is not for another two weeks. You are still working on your analysis, though at this point you are quite certain your value opinion will fall between $18 and $22 million. You have not yet begun to write the report. Your client, Client M, calls and asks whether you can provide "some idea of the value" at this point. He wants it in writing, and he wants it by this afternoon.

The Consultation

After further discussion, you learn that if the client knew that your opinion of value was at least $16 million, he could move forward with an important step involving contracting for construction of the off-site improvements. Since you have already completed enough analysis to conclude that the value is at least $16 million (you're quite certain your value opinion will be between $18 and $22 million), you can meet the client's needs. You would be providing another assignment—sort of an "assignment within an assignment."

This assignment could be reported in a Restricted Use Appraisal Report, as the client is the only intended user and does not need any detail about the valuation process at this point.

Identification of the Problem

Client: Client M

Intended User: Client M

Intended Use: To assist the client in making a decision regarding contracting for construction of off-site improvements

Type of Opinion: Market value, according to definition in *The Dictionary of Real Estate Appraisal.* The objective of the appraisal is to develop an opinion as to whether the market value is at least $16 million.

Effective Date: Current date

Relevant Characteristics About the Subject: The proposed development consisting of (describe property type) located at the SW corner of State Highways 1 and 2, Anytown. Fee simple interest.

Assignment Conditions: None

Scope of Work Plan

Based on the intended use and purpose of this "assignment within an assignment," the scope of work will be very narrow. In conjunction with the "main" assignment, the data collection and analysis process has already been completed. That is, you already know that the subject is worth in excess of the benchmark amount of $16 million.

Scope of Work Discussion in Report

The value opinion expressed in this brief report was developed in the process of completing an assignment involving a broad scope of work and preparation of a self-contained appraisal report; this assignment is to be completed in approximately two weeks. The purpose of this brief report is to express whether or not the subject property is valued at least $16 million. With this information, the client will be able to make a decision about a construction contract. The data collection and analysis process were completed in conjunction with the assignment to be completed in two weeks.

Case Study 8: "Phased" Assignments

The Request

Developer A contacts you for assistance in determining the feasibility of a proposed commercial development. He wants to know the approximate values of two alternative proposals: a smaller building of very high quality, and a larger building with few high-end features. Once he has decided between the alternatives, he would like a more thorough valuation of the project to present to investment partners.

The Consultation

Sometimes phasing assignments meets a client's needs best. From the appraiser's viewpoint, this can make good business sense also. Using this method, the appraiser and client agree that the initial assignment will involve a more narrow scope of work, enough so that the client can make an initial decision or a decision about a preliminary course of action (e.g., pursue a zoning change, proceed with development plans, or proceed from negotiation to litigation in a taking situation.) Depending on the outcome, the appraiser and client might agree to a subsequent assignment involving a more thorough scope of work.

Note that it is the client's decision making that is "preliminary"; the appraisal is completed according to USPAP and in a manner that produces a credible value opinion based on the intended use, intended user(s), and purpose of the assignment.

The appraiser must be careful in such situations to avoid even the appearance of agreeing to provide a predetermined conclusion in order to ensure a subsequent event (i.e., the follow-up assignment, which might carry with it a more substantial fee).

Identification of the Problem

Client: Developer A

Intended User: Developer A

Intended Use: First assignment: To assist in determining the feasibility of two alternative projects. Subsequent assignment: To assist in making an investment decision. (Note: This second assignment could not be for use by a regulated lender, because such a lender could not accept an appraisal engaged by the borrower.)

Type of Opinion: Market value, according to definition in *The Dictionary of Real Estate Appraisal,* for both assignments

Effective Date: Date of completion (prospective dates) for both assignments

Relevant Characteristics About the Subject: Commercial developments as described by developer

Assignment Conditions: In each assignment, the extraordinary assumption that the improvements are completed as described.

Scope of Work Plan

First Assignment
Drive by vacant site. Examine information supplied by developer about the two proposals. Careful analysis of supply and demand and market

area trends will be important. Research and analyze comparable information from files and published data sources. Apply the income approach and cost approaches.

Scope of Work Discussion in Report

Disclosure of Scope of Work in the First Report

I completed an inspection of the subject site from the current access. I was provided with conceptual plans from the developer of the Happy Valley project. I relied on sales and rental and expense data that I had readily available to me or that I had uncovered in recent assignments involving similar types of properties.

To arrive at preliminary cost estimates for the two alternative properties, I reviewed the cost estimates supplied by the developer and compared them with development costs from previously analyzed similar projects.

The assignment results developed are intended to be used solely by the client in determining which of two proposed projects will bring the greatest economic return. Because the client's intended use is preliminary, a more thorough investigation of the values of the two proposed projects was not deemed to be necessary.

Case Study 9: Market Rent Opinion

The Request

Tenant A contacts you about getting a market rent opinion for the space he is leasing.

The Consultation

Tenant A explains that his lease is up for renegotiation, but he thinks the rent the landlord wants may be too high. It's a 5,000-sq.-ft. retail space in a six-tenant strip retail center anchored by a regional grocery chain. You clarify: You will develop an opinion of "market rent," based on triple net lease terms. This is technically an "appraisal" (opinion of value) under USPAP. The client says he doesn't need a lot of detail–"just the number." You determine, based on this conversation, that a restricted use appraisal report would be appropriate, as it is for the client's use only, and he does not need much detail.

Identification of the Problem

Client: Tenant A

Intended User: Tenant A

Intended Use: To assist the client in renegotiating his lease

Type of Opinion: Market rent, according to definition in *The Dictionary of Real Estate Appraisal*

Effective Date: Current date

Relevant Characteristics About the Subject: Lease interest in the 5,000-sq.-ft. retail space located at 123 Main St., Unit B.

Assignment Conditions: None.

Scope of Work Plan

Visit subject property to obtain relevant property characteristics. Check any restrictions on use with the lease and planning department.

Search for comparable rentals in local listing service and by contacting leasing agents and property managers who work with this property type in this market area.

Scope of Work Discussion in Report

I visually inspected the subject premises on mm/dd/yy and took note of amenities and features important to the typical user of this type of space. I researched restrictions on use with the local land use jurisdiction, and analyzed current supply and demand conditions. I examined lease terms and conditions typically encountered in the local market. I investigated recently signed leases of similar space, and analyzed current listings for available space. Using this information, I completed a rental comparison analysis to arrive at a conclusion of market rent for the subject property.

Case Study 10: Portfolio Evaluation

The Request

Party Y needs an appraisal of an investment portfolio consisting of 15 apartment complexes across five states. Party Y has four days to decide whether to purchase an interest in this portfolio.

The Consultation

You discuss the nature of this type of assignment with the client. Portfolio evaluation assignments involve developing value opinions for a number of properties held in a single investment portfolio. The client's question concerns a group of properties either being sold or financed in bulk. The properties typically vary in location and use, though often they are of the same type.

Inevitably, clients in this sort of situation are under severe time constraints; they must make their decision given the best available information. Thus, they are usually willing to accept the risk associated with an appraisal that is based on an extremely narrow scope of work.

Identification of the Problem

Client: Party Y

Intended User: Party Y

Intended Use: To assist the client in making a decision regarding investing in a portfolio

Type of Opinion: Market value according to definition in *The Dictionary of Real Estate Appraisal*

Effective Date: Current date

Relevant Characteristics About the Subject: The 15 apartment complexes, as described in information provided by the client.

Assignment Conditions: Extraordinary assumptions: That the information about the unit type, size, condition, quality, amenities, and other relevant features provided by the client is accurate, and that information about factors affecting value such as economic trends and supply and demand is accurate.

Scope of Work Plan

The assignment will be made based on several extraordinary assumptions. No physical inspection will be made of the properties. Readily available information about factors affecting value such as economic trends will be relied upon. Readily available data (sales, rental, expense, capitalization, and discount rates) will be relied upon. The income approach only will be used to analyze the property values.

Scope of Work Discussion in Report

No physical inspection was made of the properties included in the subject portfolio. Information about the unit type, size, condition, quality, amenities, and other relevant features was provided by the client. This assignment is based on the extraordinary assumption that this information is accurate.

I relied upon readily available information about factors affecting value such as economic trends and supply and demand. The assignment is based on the extraordinary assumption that the information analyzed is accurate.

I relied on sales, rental, expense, capitalization, and discount rates that were readily available in my appraisal company's files. I also referred to the XXX Report, a real estate publication that provides quarterly surveys of apartment sales data including capitalization and discount rates.

Only the income approach was found to be relevant to this assignment. The sales comparison and cost approaches were not used.

When taking on a review assignment, it is absolutely critical that the appraiser and the client are on the same wavelength regarding the nature of the assignment. "Review" does not mean the same thing to all people, for the appraisal review process can proceed in a great variety of ways, depending on the scope of work applied.

USPAP's Standard 3, which addresses appraisal review, requires that the reviewer identify the scope of work and properly disclose it in the appraisal review report.

The subject of an appraisal review assignment can involve all of an appraisal report or any part of a report. It can also involve a workfile, a portion of a workfile, or some combination of workfile and report. Any "work" prepared by an appraiser can be reviewed.

Field review and desk review are two common terms used to identify the level of inspection for the subject of the appraisal assignment. These terms are too generic to use in describing what you did (or did not do) in a particular assignment.

Because the intended use of an appraisal review assignment can vary, so can the scope of work. A review for quality control most likely will have a different scope of work than a review undertaken for a second opinion of value.

The following examples illustrate two levels of work in two different appraisal review assignments.

Case Study 11: Appraisal Review—Narrow Scope

The Request

Attorney B asks you to point out the weaknesses in an appraisal report involved in litigation.

The Consultation

You suggest to the client–and he agrees–that you should identify both the strengths and the weaknesses. Otherwise, you would be producing a biased opinion. Furthermore, you are better serving this client by giving him full information about the quality of the work under review.

You confirm that the client is not looking for your opinion of the value of the property that is subject of the work under review. Rather, his concern is with the reasonableness of the appraiser's methodology as presented in the report.

Identification of the Problem

Client: Attorney B

Intended User: Attorney B

Intended Use: To assist the client in making a decision regarding the usefulness of an appraisal prepared for litigation purposes

Type of Opinion: The quality of the work under review

Effective Date: Current date

Relevant Characteristics About the Subject: The appraisal report prepared by (name of appraiser) dated mm/dd/yy of the property located at 123 Main St

Assignment Conditions: None

Scope of Work Plan

Read report, check math, check against USPAP reporting requirements, and consider adequacy of appraiser's reasoning and support.

Scope of Work Discussion in Report

As the reviewer, I did not inspect the subject property or the comparables. All information about the subject property was taken from the appraisal report under review, prepared by (name of appraiser) dated mm/dd/yy, which was provided by the client. The report included XX pages, including addenda. As reviewer, I did not research any additional data, as agreed upon with the client, based on the intended use. I reviewed the entire appraisal report for content, analysis, and methodology as well as for compliance with USPAP.

Case Study 12: Appraisal Review–Broad Scope

The Request

Party O asks you to review an appraisal of a multitenant industrial building, which he is considering buying.

The Consultation

The seller has provided Party O with an appraisal of the property that was prepared for the seller. Party O needs a comprehensive review of this appraisal with an indication of whether the reviewer agrees with the value. If the reviewer does not agree, then Party O needs you, the reviewer, to develop an appropriate opinion of value for the subject property. In developing your opinion, you will consider the data presented in the appraisal report but may research the market for additional data as well.

Identification of the Problem

Client: Party O

Intended User: Party O

Intended Use: To assist in negotiating the sale price of the real estate

Type of Opinion: To confirm the market value opinion expressed in the work under review

Effective Date: Current date

Relevant Characteristics About the Subject: The appraisal report prepared by (name of appraiser) dated mm/dd/yy of the property located at 123 Main St

Assignment Conditions: None

Scope of Work Plan

- View subject of the appraisal
- Read report
- Check math
- Check USPAP reporting requirements
- Research additional sales
- Verify all sales
- Consider adequacy of appraiser's reasoning and support
- Re-run cash flow
- Re-analyze sales and income approaches if they disagree with appraiser

Scope of Work Discussion in Report

I have read the appraisal report prepared by (name of appraiser) for Party O dated mm/dd/yy. I checked all mathematical calculations and verified that all sales and income information has been verified for accuracy. I re-ran the cash flow analysis after reconsidering the assumptions and data given. I analyzed the appraisal for compliance with the Uniform Standards of Professional Appraisal Practice (USPAP).

I inspected the interior and exterior of the subject property on mm/dd/yy. I researched the state industrial sales database to locate additional sales and/or income information from the period mm/dd/yy to mm/dd/yy. I verified all data with one of the parties to the transaction.

The sections of the appraisal under review that are accurate and in compliance with USPAP have been included as part of this review appraisal. Those areas that are either not in compliance or not accurate are not included as part of this review, and I have completed a new analysis of those sections (state which sections).

Chapter 10

In order for a set of rules to be applicable to a broad variety of situations, they must be sufficiently flexible. If they lack flexibility, they may quickly lose relevance and become prone to being disregarded. There cannot be rules simply for the sake of having rules. Rules must be purposeful; they must serve to promote good causes, not impede them.

The flexibility mechanism in USPAP is scope of work. The phrase scope of work made its way into USPAP in 1999, but effective July 2006, USPAP has been significantly overhauled so that the concept pervades it entirely. While the text of USPAP may be changed significantly, its content has not. The key difference is in how USPAP views the appraisal problem. Under the prior flexibility mechanism–the Departure Rule–an appraisal was either complete or limited, depending on whether or not all of the standards rules were followed. In this way of thinking, the "ideal" assignment was the one with the most; that is, the fewer exceptions, the better.

Using the new scope of work concept, solving the client's "problem to be solved" is a three step process. First, the appraiser must identify the problem. Second, the appraiser must plan the solution. And third, the appraiser must apply the solution to arrive at credible results. In effect, for every appraisal problem, there is an "ideal" solution set–and that solution step will include all steps necessary to arrive at credible results, given the intended use and the intended user. Steps that aren't necessary don't need to be completed. This model is the same model used in many other professions. In fact, the hallmark of a true professional is the ability to diagnose a problem and propose a reasonable means to find a solution.

The first step, identifying the problem, is carried out by identifying the significant seven–client, intended users, intended use, type of opinion, effective date of opinion, relevant characteristics about the subject, and assignment conditions. The second step, planning the solution (or scope of work) requires the appraiser to be competent with regard to that type of problem. The appraisal process can be "sliced and diced" many different ways. The appraiser's job is to figure out what will need to be done to solve the particular problem at hand, keeping in mind that the goal–always–is credible results.

The appraiser must be prepared to support the scope of work decision and, in any report, must clearly disclose the scope of work applied in the assignment. While USPAP does not dictate the form or format of such a discussion, the appraiser must be careful to be clear, not misleading, and sufficiently descriptive.

Scope of work gives appraisers the ability to customize assignments in order to better serve their clients. In an ever-changing business environment, and an expanding global economy, such flexibility is increasingly important. Scope of work allows appraisers to expand their range of services beyond the traditional ones and opens doors to new opportunities.

Summary Appraisal Report Format

The following is a guideline with examples for preparing a summary appraisal report.

This guideline is intended to assist in the understanding of the requirements of the *Uniform Standards of Professional Appraisal Practice* (USPAP) relating to summary appraisal reports and has been developed for educational and illustrative purposes only. While the Appraisal Institute uses reasonable efforts to provide helpful information in this Summary Appraisal Report Format, the Appraisal Institute makes no representations or warranties as to the accuracy, reliability, or completeness of the information contained herein, or whether following the format is appropriate for any particular appraisal assignment, will result in compliance with client requirements, or will result in compliance with applicable laws or regulations, including but not limited to USPAP. The Appraisal Institute provides this Summary Appraisal Report Format with the understanding that it is not providing legal, accounting, or other professional advice. The Appraisal Institute urges you to work closely with your clients regarding client requirements and to contact the appropriate jurisdiction and professionals for interpretation and application of USPAP requirements relating to summary appraisal reports.

Some appraisers might use this type of format by itself, while others might also include a letter of transmittal. Remember, an appraiser must retain a workfile for each assignment.

Client

State the identity of the client by name. USPAP allows you to state the client's identity by type rather than by name, but this would only be necessary in the rare instances in which the client wishes to remain anonymous. The client is the person, entity, or entities that hire you in an assignment.

> Mr. John Q. Owner
> 1234 Main St.
> Anytown, USA 00000

Subject Property

Provide an address or other brief means of identifying the subject.

> 200 Wakefield Lane
> Anytown, USA

Intended Users

Intended users are those you identify as users of the report. You make this determination based on your communication with the client, and you make it at the time you take the assignment. Intended users are the ones to whom you are responsible for ensuring that the report is understandable; i.e., when you write the report, remember that the intended users are your audience.

> Client and others as appropriate

Intended Use

Possible intended uses include:
- Establishing a price at which to buy
- Establishing a price at which to sell
- Making a decision regarding financing
- Establishing a basis for taxation
- Establishing the terms of a lease
- Financial reporting
- Tax reporting
- The preliminary analysis of just compensation in eminent domain proceedings
- Establishing the value of a charitable donation
- A divorce settlement
- A portfolio analysis
- Establishing a fair partnership value

- Estate planning/settlement
- Other

Interest Valued

State whether the interest appraised is the fee simple, leased fee, lease-hold, or some other interest. You might also want to identify the party who holds the interest appraised.

Leased fee

Purpose of the Assignment

The type of value is stated and the definition is given. Be sure to cite the source of the definition.

To develop an opinion of market value of the above-stated interest in the subject property. Market value is defined as follows:

The most probable price which a property should bring in a competitive and open market under all conditions requisite to a fair sale, the buyer and seller each acting prudently and knowledgeably, and assuming the price is not affected by undue stimulus. Implicit in this definition is the consummation of a sale as of a specified date and the passing of title from seller to buyer under conditions whereby:

1. buyer and seller are typically motivated;
2. both parties are well informed or well advised, and acting in what they consider their own best interests;
3. a reasonable time is allowed for exposure in the open market;
4. payment is made in terms of cash in United States dollars or in terms of financial arrangements comparable thereto; and
5. the price represents the normal consideration for the property sold unaffected by special or creative financing or sales concessions granted by anyone associated with the sale.

(*The Dictionary of Real Estate Appraisal*, 4th edition, Appraisal Institute, 2002.)

This example is a commonly used market value definition. However, the value need not be market value; it could be use value, insurable value, or investment value. Regardless, include the definition and cite its source. If the value developed is market value, and it is NOT in terms of cash or based on financing terms equivalent to cash, summarize the terms of the financing and explain the influence on value.

Opinion of Value

Self-explanatory

$1,290,000

Extraordinary Assumptions

An extraordinary assumption is something that is assumed to be true, but that is not certain. If it turns out to be untrue, the value conclusion would be impacted. Extraordinary assumptions are those assumptions that are specific to the particular assignment (e.g., that a possibly contaminated site is not adversely impacted by contamination), as opposed to general assumptions, which could be applicable to any assignment (e.g., that the title is marketable).

None

Hypothetical Conditions

Hypothetical conditions are known to be false but are presumed to be true for the purpose of reasonable analysis. For example, if the property is appraised as of today as though the improvements were complete, but the property currently consists of a vacant site, the valuation of the improved property would be subject to the hypothetical condition that the improvements are complete.

None

Effective Date of Value Opinion

The effective date of value is the date on which the opinion of value is relevant. It could be either a current date, a retrospective date, or a prospective date.

January 1, 2003

Date of Report

The date of the report is the date on which the report is prepared. If the report is prepared over a period of time, the date that it is finalized, or the date that it is given or sent to the client, should be used.

February 1, 2003

Scope of Work

The scope of work applied in the development of the appraisal is summarized.

In preparing this appraisal, the appraiser

- inspected the subject site and the exterior of the improvements as well as the interior of 15 of the 40 units;
- gathered information on comparable land and improved sales, rents, operating expenses, construction costs, depreciation, and capitalization and yield rates;
- confirmed all comparable sales and rental information with at least one of the parties to the transaction;
- analyzed the data and applied the sales comparison, cost, and income capitalization approaches. In the income capitalization approach, the appraiser used gross rent multiplier analysis as well as direct capitalization and yield capitalization (DCF analysis).

Report Option

This report is a Summary Appraisal Report in accordance with Standards Rule 2-2(b) of the *Uniform Standards of Professional Appraisal Practice.* As such, it presents sufficient information to enable the client and other intended users, as identified, to understand it properly.

Summary Description of the Real Estate Appraised

The property's physical and economic characteristics that are relevant to the appraisal problem are summarized. Include sufficient information to enable the client and intended users to understand these characteristics and their relevance to the appraisal problem. Information about sales that occurred within the three years before the effective date of value must be included as well as information about current listings, options, or agreements of sale (unless it is unavailable).

Market Area: Anytown is a suburban community approximately 20 miles west of Big City. Many residents of Anytown commute to work in Big City. Housing in Anytown tends to be more affordable than in areas closer to Big City. Demand for housing in Anytown has been increasingly strong during the last decade, while the supply of both single-family and multifamily residential properties has increased commensurately. Very little vacant land remains available for additional development in the subject's immediate area; most new development is now taking place on the outskirts of Anytown. The economic outlook for both the immediate future and over the long term for the Big City Metropolitan Statistical Area (MSA) is favorable. Household income and population are expected to continue to grow.

The subject's neighborhood is developed predominantly with two-story, garden-style apartments built between 8 and 15 years ago. Most complexes have between 25 and 50 units, are of average quality construction, and are generally well maintained. Vacancy has ranged between 2% and 4% during the last three years. Demand for two-bedroom units is considerably stronger than for one-bedroom units. Two-bedroom units generally rent for about $400 to $500 per month; one-bedroom units rent for about $300 to $400 per month. Tenants typically pay for electricity. Complexes without covered parking, which tend to be the older complexes in the neighborhood, are somewhat more difficult to lease and achieve about $20 per unit per month less in rent.

The subject complex conforms well to surrounding land uses. Its location on Wakefield Lane provides adequate visibility. Traffic volume on Wakefield Lane is moderate and does not negatively impact the subject's locational appeal or ability to compete with other complexes in this area. Schools, one convenience food market, and recreational facilities are within walking distance. Other shopping and services are a 5- to 10-minute drive away.

Property Description: The subject site is rectangular with 225 feet of frontage on the west side of Wakefield Lane. Gross (and usable) area is one acre (43,560 square feet). The site is essentially level, and soil conditions appear to be typical of the area. The property is not located in a FEMA-identified special flood hazard area, and it is not in a seismic zone. The site is zoned R2, which allows multifamily residential development with a maximum density of 40 units per acre.

The subject improvements consist of four two-story wood frame buildings, each with 10 single-level apartment units, a laundry room, and a recreation room. Gross building area is 32,000 square feet. The buildings are wood sided and have flat tar-and-gravel roofs. All of the units have two bedrooms and one bath, and contain approximately 700 square feet of living area. The improvements are of average quality construction and maintenance is generally good. Actual age and effective age are 10 years. Unit and project amenities are typical for this area. There are 40 carport parking spaces and 20 open parking spaces. This ratio is typical for complexes in this area.

The property appraised includes drapes and refrigerators in each unit. This personal property is not considered significant to the overall value of the property.

All of the units are currently leased under written leases. Lease terms range from three to six months.

The property is legally described as Lot 7 of Block 2, recorded in Book 37 at page 29 of Maps, Records of Big City County, USA. A title report dated December 1, 1995, prepared by GOK Title Company, shows no known easements or encumbrances.

According to public records, title to the subject property has been in the name of Adam Smith for 10 years. No current listings, options, or agreements of sale of the subject property were discovered in the course of this analysis.

Highest and Best Use Analysis

Whenever the purpose of the appraisal is to develop an opinion of market value, the support and rationale for the opinion of the highest and best use of the real estate must be summarized. The highest and best use of the site as though vacant and the highest and best use of the property as it is currently improved must be addressed. If the appraisal is of proposed improvements, the highest and best use of the property if improved as proposed should be addressed.

> Highest and best use as though vacant: The only legally permissible use of the subject site is multifamily residential with a density of up to 40 units per acre. The likelihood of a zoning change is remote. The only legally possible use that is also physically possible would be a two-story complex with up to 40 units ranging in size from 650 to 750 square feet with at least 1.5 parking spaces per unit. Such a complex would be financially feasible if it were operated as a rental complex; condominium ownership would not be feasible at this time. Thus, the maximally productive and highest and best use of the subject site as though vacant would be a two-story rental apartment complex with 40 units.
>
> Highest and best use as improved: Neither demolition of the existing improvements and redevelopment of the subject site, nor modification of the existing improvements would result in a higher return to the land than is currently being achieved. The existing apartment complex is therefore concluded to be the highest and best use as improved.

Valuation Analysis

The information analyzed, the appraisal procedures followed, and the reasoning that supports the analyses, opinions, and conclusions are summarized. Sufficient information so the client and intended users can understand the rationale for the opinion and conclusions should be included. If there were sales of the property in the three years before the effective date of value, they should be included in the analysis. Current listings, contracts, or options on the property should be included in the analysis (unless the information is not available, in which case, it should be stated). Remember, the appraiser must provide sufficient information to enable the client and intended users to understand the rationale.

With a sales comparison approach, if minor adjustments that are made for age and condition amount to more than 3% per adjustment, a brief discussion on how they were calculated should be included.

If rental comparables adjustments amount to more than 35% per adjustment, a brief discussion on how they were calculated should also be included.

If yield analysis were given more weight than in the example below, more discussion would be warranted.

Sales Comparison Approach: A summary of the data on comparable improved sales is illustrated below.

Sale No.	Address	Sale Price	Date of Sale	No. of Units	GBA (SF)	$/ Unit	$/SF GBA	EGIM	OAR
1	Cozy Acres 1221 Tinker St.	$1,420,000	10/95	49	38,400	$28,980	$36.98	6.01	9.98%
2	The Embassador 900 Tailer St.	$1,300,000	7/95	42	34,000	$30,952	$38.24	6.22	9.75%
3	Colonial Manor 1751 Soldier St.	$1,090,000	1/95	32	26,000	$34,062	$41.92	6.14	9.77%

Three sales of similar apartment complexes in the subject's neighborhood were analyzed. These sales all occurred within the last year. The complexes range in size from 32 to 49 units, and in age from 8 to 12 years. Sale prices range from approximately $29,000 to $34,000 per unit, and from approximately $37 to $42 per square foot of gross building area. When minor adjustments are made for age and condition, the sales indicate a value of $31,000 per unit for the subject, or $1,240,000. On a square-foot basis, the adjusted sales indicate a value of $40 per square foot for the subject, or $1,280,000. More reliance was placed on the price per unit because investors in this type of property in this location rarely consider price per square foot.

Cost Approach: Replacement cost information was gathered from recently constructed apartment complexes of similar quality in the greater Big City area. Depreciation was extracted from sales of comparable properties. The value of the site as though vacant was estimated using the sales comparison approach, and three sales of parcels with similar locations and zoning were analyzed. A summary of the land sales analyzed is illustrated below.

Sale No.	Location	Sale Price	Date of Sale	Allowable Units	$/Allowable Unit
1	101 Long Rd.	$224,000	11/95	40	$5,600
2	7800 Middle Rd.	$235,000	5/95	42	$5,595
3	290 Short Rd.	$226,000	2/95	40	$5,650

The value indicated by the cost approach is summarized as follows:

Replacement cost estimate

32,000 SF @ $40/SF	$1,280,000
Paving	30,000
Carports	100,000
RCN	$1,410,000
Less depreciation from all sources	352,000
DRCN	$1,058,000
Plus site value	225,000
Indicated value	$1,283,000

Income Capitalization Approach: A rental survey of 12 similar apartment complexes in the subject's neighborhood and similar neighborhoods in the Anytown area indicated that two-bedroom apartment units rent for about $400 to $500 per month. Two-bedroom units at Highland Manor, located just south of the subject, currently rent for $440 to $445 per month. This complex is very similar to the subject but is in inferior condition. Two-bedroom units at The Flatlands, located across the street from the subject and also very similar, rent for $455 to $470 per month. Two-bedroom units at The Village rent for $480 to $490 per month. The Village is slightly superior to the subject in that its amenities include a heated swimming pool and tennis courts.

Rental comparables, when adjusted for condition and unit amenities, indicate a market rental for the subject's two-bedroom units of $460 per month, which approximates the actual rents under the current leases. Vacancy and expense information is based on data gathered on comparable properties in the area. Comparable sales indicate overall capitalization rates of 9.75% to 10%. Surveys of investors in this type of property indicate that the desired property yield rate is about 13%.

The income capitalization approach using direct capitalization is summarized as follows:

Gross income 40 × $460 × 12	$220,800
Less 5% vacancy & collection	11,040
Effective gross income	$209,760
Less operating expenses	83,904
Net operating income	$125,856
OAR	9.75%
Indicated value, rounded	$1,290,000

Yield capitalization was also applied. A 13% property yield rate was used, based on discussion with investors in the local market as well as published surveys of investors and other market participants. Income and expenses were expected to grow at 4% per year for a 10-year holding period. The resulting value indication using this technique is $1,310,000, rounded. Yield analysis is given less weight than direct capitalization because it is not reflective of the decision-making process of the typical investor in this property type.

Effective gross income multipliers for the comparables analyzed in the sales comparison approach range from 0.01 to 6.22. Applying an EGIM of 6.15 to the subject's effective gross income of $209,760 indicates a value of $1,290,000, rounded. This supports the value indicated using direct capitalization.

Reconciliation and Value Conclusion: The income capitalization approach using direct capitalization is given the most weight because of the quality and quantity of the rental and expense information that could be obtained, as well as the availability and consistency of GIMs and capitalization rates obtained from the market. The sales comparison approach is given less weight, although investors do consider price per unit in their decision-making process.

The market value of the subject property, as of the effective date, is therefore estimated to be $1,290,000.

The improved property sales indicated that exposure time (i.e., the length of time the subject property would have been exposed for sale in the market had it sold at the market value concluded in this analysis as of the date of this valuation) would have been about 10 months. The estimated marketing time (i.e., the amount of time it would probably take to sell the subject property if exposed in the market beginning on the date of this valuation) is 9 to 12 months.

Certification

If more than one appraiser signs the report, this certification can be modified so that it reads in the plural sense, or it can be duplicated and each appraiser can sign a separate certification.

I certify that, to the best of my knowledge and belief:

- The statements of fact contained in this report are true and correct.
- The reported analyses, opinions, and conclusions are limited only by the reported assumptions and limiting conditions and are my personal, impartial, and unbiased professional analyses, opinions, and conclusions.
- I have no (or the specified) present or prospective interest in the property that is the subject of this report and no (or the specified) personal interest with respect to the parties involved.
- I have no bias with respect to the property that is the subject of this report or to the parties involved with this assignment.
- My engagement in this assignment was not contingent upon developing or reporting predetermined results.
- My compensation for completing this assignment is not contingent upon the development or reporting of a predetermined value or direction in value that favors the cause of the client, the amount of the value opinion, the attainment of a stipulated result, or the occurrence of a subsequent event directly related to the intended use of this appraisal.
- My analyses, opinions, and conclusions were developed, and this report has been prepared, in conformity with the *Uniform Standards of Professional Appraisal Practice.*
- I have (or have not) made a personal inspection of the property that is the subject of this report. (if more than one person signs this certification, the certification must clearly specify which individuals did and which individuals did not make a personal inspection of the appraised property.)
- No one provided significant real property appraisal assistance to the person signing this certification. (if there are exceptions, the name of each individual providing significant real property appraisal assistance must be stated.)

Appraisal Institute members must certify to the following:

- I certify that, to the best of my knowledge and belief, the reported analyses, opinions, and conclusions were developed, and this report has been prepared, in conformity with the requirements of the code of professional ethics and standards of professional appraisal practice of the Appraisal Institute.
- I certify that the use of this report is subject to the requirements of the Appraisal Institute relating to review by its duly authorized representatives.

Designated members of the Appraisal Institute must certify that:

- As of the date of this report, I (or designated member's name or designated members' names) have/has completed the continuing education program of the Appraisal Institute.

or

- As of the date of this report, I (or designated member's name or designated members' names) have not/has not completed the continuing education program of the Appraisal Institute.

Restricted Use Appraisal Report Format

This guideline is intended to assist in the understanding of the requirements of the *Uniform Standards of Professional Appraisal Practice* (USPAP) relating to restricted use appraisal reports and has been developed for educational and illustrative purposes only. While the Appraisal Institute uses reasonable efforts to provide helpful information in this Restricted Use Appraisal Report Format, it makes no representations or warranties as to the accuracy, reliability or completeness of the information contained herein, or that following this format for any particular appraisal assignment will result in compliance with client requirements, or will result in compliance with applicable laws or regulations, including but not limited to USPAP. The Appraisal Institute provides this Restricted Use Appraisal Report Format with the understanding that it is not providing legal, accounting, or other professional advice. The Appraisal Institute urges you to work closely with your clients regarding client requirements and to contact the appropriate jurisdiction and professionals for interpretation and application of USPAP requirements relating to restricted use appraisal reports.

An appraiser might use this type of format by itself, while others might also include a letter of transmittal. Remember, an appraiser must retain a workfile for each assignment. The workfile must contain sufficient information so that if asked, the appraiser could create a summary appraisal report from it later (i.e., any time during the prescribed record retention period, which is a minimum of 5 years).

Client/Intended User

An appraiser would state the identity of the client by name. USPAP allows an appraiser to state the client's identity by type rather than by name, but for a restricted use appraisal report this will rarely be necessary. IMPORTANT: A restricted use appraisal report may be used ONLY if the client is the sole intended user. An appraiser MUST ascertain with the client at the time the appraiser takes the assignment that the client is the sole intended user. The client is the person, entity, or entities that hire the appraiser in an assignment. If the client consists of more than one person, they must be acting together to make a single decision in their use of this appraisal.

Mr. John Q. Owner
1234 Main St.
Anytown, USA 00000

Intended Use

Possible intended uses include:

- Establishing a price at which to buy
- Establishing a price at which to sell
- Making a decision regarding financing
- Establishing a basis for taxation
- Establishing the terms of a lease
- Financial reporting
- Tax reporting
- The preliminary analysis of just compensation in eminent domain proceedings
- Establishing the value of a charitable donation
- A divorce settlement
- A portfolio analysis
- Establishing a fair partnership value
- Estate planning/settlement

For the sole use by the client in establishing a price at which to sell. This report is not intended for any other use. The appraiser is not responsible for unauthorized use of this report.

Identification of Real Estate

In a restricted use appraisal report, no description of the property is provided. Rather, only a brief statement is made that is adequate to identify the particular piece of real estate involved. In most cases, the property address will suffice. In other cases, a legal description will be appropriate. In rare instances, an appraiser could use a map reference, or reference an attached copy of a survey map or photographs.

100 West Ave., Anytown, USA

Current Use

Self-explanatory

Multitenant office building

Highest and Best Use

If the purpose of the assignment is to develop an opinion of some kind of market value, the conclusion of the highest and best use of the real estate must be stated. In a restricted use appraisal report, no explanation is provided as to how the appraiser arrived at this conclusion. However, support must be retained in the appraiser's workfile. An appraiser must be sure to have enough information in his or her workfile about the conclusion of highest and best use so that the he or she can later write a summary appraisal report, if asked.

Current use

Real Property Interest Valued

Possible interests include fee simple, leased fee, leasehold, and others.

Fee simple

Purpose of the Assignment

The type of value is stated and the source of its definition is given. There is no need to include the definition itself in a restricted use appraisal report.

To develop an opinion of the market value as defined by the agencies that regulate financial institutions in the United States and published by the Appraisal Institute in *The Dictionary of Real Estate Appraisal*, 4th edition, 2002.

Effective Date of Value Opinion

The effective date of value is the date on which the opinion of value is relevant. It could be a current date, a retrospective date, or a prospective date.

January 1, 2003

Date of Report

The date of the report is the date on which the report is prepared. If the report is prepared over a period of time, the appraiser would use the date that it is finalized, or the date that the report is given or sent to the client.

February 1, 2003

Scope of Work

The appraiser would state the extent of the process of collecting, confirming, and reporting data. The appraiser would state whether any of the usual valuation approaches were excluded. Alternatively, the appraiser could reference an assignment agreement (e.g., engagement letter) in the appraiser's workfile that details the scope of work.

Refer to the appraiser's engagement letter to the client dated December 15, 2002. A copy of this letter is retained in the appraiser's workfile.

Report Option

Self-explanatory

This report is a Restricted Use Appraisal Report in accordance with Standards Rule 2-2(c) of the *Uniform Standards of Professional Appraisal Practice.* As such, it presents no discussions of the data, reasoning, and analyses that were used in the appraisal process to develop the appraiser's opinion of value. Supporting documentation concerning the data, reasoning, and analyses is retained in the appraiser's file.

Extraordinary Asssumptions

An extraordinary assumption is something that is assumed to be true, but that is not certain. If it turns out to be untrue, the value conclusion would be impacted. Extraordinary assumptions are those assumptions that are specific to the particular assignment (e.g., that a possibly contaminated site is not adversely impacted by contamination), as opposed to general assumptions, which could be applicable to any assignment (e.g., that the title is marketable).

None

Hypothetical Conditions

Hypothetical conditions are known to be false, but are presumed to be true for the purpose of reasonable analysis. For example, if the property is appraised as of today as though the improvements were complete, but the property currently consists of a vacant site, the valuation of the improved property would be subject to the hypothetical condition that the improvements are complete.

None

Opinion of Value

Self-explanatory

$1,000,000

Certification

If more than one appraiser signs the report, this certification can be modified so that it reads in the plural sense, or it can be duplicated and each appraiser can sign a separate certification. If more than one person signs this certification, the certification must clearly specify which individuals did and which did not make a personal inspection of the appraised property. If there are exceptions, the name of each individual providing significant real property appraisal assistance must be stated.

I certify that, to the best of my knowledge and belief:

- The statements of fact contained in this report are true and correct.
- The reported analyses, opinions, and conclusions are limited only by the reported assumptions and limiting conditions and are my personal, impartial, and unbiased professional analyses, opinions, and conclusions.
- I have no present or prospective interest in the property that is the subject of this report and no personal interest with respect to the parties involved.
- I have no bias with respect to the property that is the subject of this report or to the parties involved with this assignment.
- My engagement in this assignment was not contingent upon developing or reporting predetermined results.
- My compensation for completing this assignment is not contingent upon the development or reporting of a predetermined value or direction in value that favors the cause of the client, the amount of the value opinion, the attainment of a stipulated result, or the occurrence of a subsequent event directly related to the intended use of this appraisal.
- My analyses, opinions, and conclusions were developed, and this report has been prepared, in conformity with the *Uniform Standards of Professional Appraisal Practice.*
- I have made a personal inspection of the property that is the subject of this report.
- No one provided significant real property appraisal assistance to the person signing this certification.

Appraisal Institute members must certify to the following:

- I certify that, to the best of my knowledge and belief, the reported analyses, opinions, and conclusions were developed, and this report has been prepared, in conformity with the requirements of the code of professional ethics and standards of professional appraisal practice of the Appraisal Institute.
- I certify that the use of this report is subject to the requirements of the Appraisal Institute relating to review by its duly authorized representatives.

Designated members of the Appraisal Institute must certify that:

- As of the date of this report, I (or designated member's name or designated members' names) have/has completed the continuing education program of the Appraisal Institute.

or

- As of the date of this report, I (or designated member's name or designated members' names) have not/has not completed the continuing education program of the Appraisal Institute.